How to
Feel Good
in Difficult
Times

GAEL LINDENFIELD

TRIGGER
The mental health & wellbeing publisher

First published in 2020
This edition published in 2023 by Trigger Publishing
An imprint of Shaw Callaghan Ltd

UK Office
The Stanley Building
7 Pancras Square
Kings Cross
London N1C 4AG

US Office
On Point Executive Center, Inc
3030 N Rocky Point Drive W
Suite 150
Tampa, FL 33607
www.triggerhub.org

A CIP catalogue record for this book is available upon request from the British
Library
ISBN: 978-1-83796-250-1
Ebook ISBN: 978-1-83796-251-8

Cover design and typeset by Georgie Hewitt

CONTENTS

....

INTRODUCTION

My ability to deal well with setbacks is a privilege that I will never take for granted. Life can feel literally hell and impossibly daunting without it. I have been lucky in that I had a chance to learn how to deal with these kinds of debilitating emotional reactions to setbacks and have had many opportunities to put them into practice in real life.

The crucial key to making the best of difficult times is, I believe, to look for the positive in change, however unwelcome it may seem. But I also know that this is much easier said than done, and that certain qualities and skills are needed to make it possible. Confidence, emotional resilience and motivation are required in order to be able to move on positively, but, by their very nature, difficult times will knock all three of these out of the best of us. I have written many self-help programmes designed to develop and strengthen them, but when a setback hits, most people have neither the time nor the energy to embark upon demanding plans for personal development.

Neuroscientists have warned that the human brain cannot evolve and adapt quickly enough to cope well with the pace of change that many of us are encountering today. Perhaps this is one of the main reasons why depression and anxiety disorders are on the increase. Faced with this and the ever more uncertain state of the world, I wanted to put together a book that offered a collection of tips and tools aimed specifically at addressing the problem of low morale during tough times – and this is the result.

Some of the tips are tried-and-tested favourite strategies which I have modified, others are new ideas. While the majority can be learnt quickly and applied immediately, some are more involved, requiring a little more time to read and understand before they can be put into effective practice. Having said that, once you have read or worked on these longer tips, the next time you are in a challenging real-life situation, you will be able to apply what you have learnt very quickly.

None of us ever knows what life has in store for us or for our family and friends, but in order to emerge from setbacks stronger and more resilient, you need to keep your morale reserves continually topped up, using these tips even when your most testing time is over. This will give you a boost should you meet more difficult times in the future, as well as equipping you to help others through theirs.

I hope you find this collection of tips helpful and inspiring.

HOME

When we are going through times of crisis our natural response is often to batten down the hatches and cocoon ourselves in our safe space which, more often than not, can be found at home. Far from wallowing or hiding from our problems, this desire to hunker down and take stock is only natural, and taking time to come to terms with what has happened and working out a strategy to accept and move past the feelings that it has thrown up is an important and healthy response. One of the knock-on effects of ignoring emotional hurt is a loss of self-confidence and, consequently, morale. Buried feelings, especially deep ones, rarely just dissolve away. They have a tendency to leak or burst out and surprise you at inconvenient moments; or they may trigger physical issues, such as a loss of energy, headaches or, more seriously, problems with your heart or immune system.

This is why it is essential to deal with the emotional impact of whatever has happened to you as quickly as you can. If you have been made redundant, are facing divorce or have lost a parent, for example, you will probably need initially all the energy, confidence and inner calm you can muster to cope with the situation. And for most of us, we feel safest and calmest at home. In this chapter, I will show you how to create a safe and nurturing space in your home that will allow you to quickly take stock of the situation, breed positivity and help you gain perspective, strength and ultimately acceptance.

The tips in this section are designed to guide you through the emotional-healing process and, importantly, to help you find the time and space to put it into action.

MAKE A DATE
WITH YOUR
DUVET

*"There is nothing like
staying at home for
real comfort."*

Jane Austen, novelist

Setting aside a day occasionally for cosseting yourself with
pure self-indulgence will give both your health and self-
esteem a boost.

Nowadays, it is a common belief that this is best achieved
by booking a day at a luxury health spa. As wonderful
as these can be, even if you can afford this kind of treat,
when you are going through a particularly difficult time, it
can be counterproductive. Spas are great venues, perhaps
for celebrations and treats, but not the best places for
emotional recovery, especially if you have financial worries.

A quiet "duvet day" in the comfort of your own home is usually much more beneficial.

The longer your duvet day is, the better will be its effects, but in practical terms, you may only be able to spare a few hours. If this is the case, it is even more important to prepare for it carefully so you can make the very most of it.

Here are some suggestions to include on your to-do list:

- Make arrangements for your home to be emptied of everyone. This is a day just for you, regardless of how close you are to others. The pleasure and healing you get from togetherness is wonderful, but different. A day of self-indulgence in solitude offers other possibilities. It gives you the freedom to be exactly who you are; think about whatever comes into your mind, however stupid, illogical or disgraceful those thoughts may seem, and, of course, to do whatever you want to do, even if that is nothing.

- If you have to ask for help to make your solitude possible, remember that you can return favours later; giving back to someone else in their hour of need is so pleasurable that you will receive a bonus mood-booster.

- Fill your fridge with nutritious bite-sized treats and healthy drinks. In particular, make sure you have all you need for a luxurious breakfast in bed, as this will put you in the correct self-indulgent mood. If you prefer to cook and prepare these yourself, do as much of the work as you can the day before. Duvet days are lazy days.

- Inform anyone who is likely to call or visit that you are having an "away day". If a little white lie is necessary, simply say in a brisk tone that you have some personal matters to attend to. This will protect your privacy, as it tends to block further questions.

- Prepare your own entertainment, so that you are not relying on daytime TV to amuse you. I have heard so many people express regrets about watching "rubbish" all day that I think it is worth having a much-loved show or film lined up and ready to watch. Old favourites with a high feel-good factor or ones that make you laugh are always a safe option.

- Select a range of music that is relaxing and also some to use at the end of your "day" to uplift your mood and energise you. Remember, this is also an opportunity for you to enjoy to your heart's content all that music that irritates or bores others in your life.

- If you love reading, buy or borrow a book that you know will absorb your attention and offer some distraction from your problems. This is not the time for self-help books or any offering possible solutions. Put these aside until your morale is stronger and you are feeling more optimistic and motivated. Your concentration is probably not at its best so all those collections of inspirational quotes, quirky facts, cartoons or jokes that usually only see the light of day at Christmas time are ideal.

- Consider buying a cheap pay-as-you-go phone and give the number to only a few people whom you would want to contact you in an emergency. This will leave you free to turn off all other communication with the outside world, not just on your duvet day, but at many other times as well.

QUICK FIX:
Take a five-minute dose of soothing silence

Research carried out by Theodore Wachs, a professor of psychological sciences at Purdue University in the US, has revealed that children who come from highly noisy or chaotic homes experience less cognitive growth, delayed language skills, have trouble mastering their environments and have increased anxiety. Other research has proved that constant noise affects both physical and mental health to such a degree that many governments now have legislation and special departments in place to control it.

In today's world, there are very few accessible places where silence can be readily found. But you can create it for yourself, even if it takes earplugs plus noise-reducing headphones and triple-glazing to do so.

ADD BURSTS
OF BEAUTY
TO YOUR LIFE

Recently, I met a friend for coffee whom I hadn't seen for a couple of months. The moment I saw her, I commented on how *great* she looked. I could see she was a bit taken aback by the intensity of my tone (she did, in fact, look years younger than when I had last seen her), and she was curious to know what it was about her that had made such an impression on me. Confronted with specifying exactly what had prompted my remark, I said perhaps it was the sparkle in her eyes, her beaming smile, glowing skin and her relaxed and easy posture, all of which formed quite a different picture from the one I had seen last time we'd met.

My friend explained that over the previous months her work had become extremely pressurised. In addition, as she was nearing retirement, she had been having major anxieties about the sudden and unexpected erosion of her pension caused by the economic downturn.

As we talked, I expected to hear some good news about a change in her circumstances. But no, her stresses were greater than ever. The conversation then moved on to sharing news about our recent activities, and it became clear what had caused such a noticeable lift in my friend's demeanour and appearance. She mentioned that she had recently spent a weekend in Paris which had set her thinking. While she was there, she had done nothing particularly special or unusual. She had just walked around, looking at buildings and visiting a few galleries. But on her return, she found that she felt very different. She said she was convinced that it was simply the beauty of Paris that had lifted her mood and relaxed her body and mind. It made her realise how little time she had been spending around beauty and that she had forgotten what a powerful tonic it is for her. Since her return, she'd been setting aside time to enjoy regular "doses" of beauty, for example, taking a walk on a cliff top with stunning views, seeing a beautifully filmed movie and going on a guided tour of a well-known gallery that opened her eyes to some striking art she had never noticed before.

No wonder my friend looked so much better! Beauty is a natural stimulator of the happiness hormones. The chemical response that it sets off within us infuses us with a sense of wellbeing. It helps muscles to relax, dulls physical pain and causes mental worries to float automatically to the back of your mind.

And, of course, as my friend found on her return home, you don't need to rush off to Paris to get this kind of fix. Beauty is always available for you to enjoy in your day-to-day life. You may simply need to make a conscious effort to notice it and allow yourself a little time to appreciate it. When you are stressed, your mind is even less likely to pick up automatically on these everyday opportunities to benefit from the restorative pleasure of beauty.

One way to counter this effect of stress is to reignite your "beauty sensors" by regularly adding new and unusual stimulants into the backdrop of your life. Of course, how you choose to do this will vary from individual to individual. I might use visually stimulating pictures, for example, while my husband is more likely to listen to an uplifting piece of music. One friend of mine would choose to feel a delicately textured fabric, while another would select a fresh fragrance from a garden.

Cheap and easy ways to add bursts of beauty to everyday life:

- Buy yourself flowers or a plant each month.

- Put a new beautiful photo on to your screen saver each week.

- Borrow an art book from the library once a week.

- Collect postcards from museums and galleries or card

shops and mount regular new art shows on your kitchen cupboards or around your desk.

- Collect different leaves and draw or press inside a book and then paste on to a card and send to friends.

- Collect delicious sounding recipes and cook a new one at least once a month.

- Gather together small pieces of fabric with different textures from remnant boxes or old clothes and make into a collage or scarf that you can feel and enjoy.

- Make a collection of stones or shells and wash and polish each in turn.

- Collect a few worms and earth in a jar and observe them for a day or so.

- Visit a butterfly museum (there is a wonderful one in Portsmouth in the UK).

- Take a walk in a rose garden and drink in each of the individual scents, one by one.

- Take a few minutes each day to notice the evolving colours and shapes of the sky.

You can get many more ideas by reading or questioning people around you on this subject. Poets and young children can be great sources of inspiration as they see wondrous beauty in things that so often become "ordinary" and go unnoticed.

After finding out what others appreciate in an object or experience, make a conscious effort to be open to sensing the beauty that is able to give them so much pleasure. It doesn't always work, but when it does I find it very exciting. There was a time I never could have imagined finding myself uplifted by the beauty of a gliding snail in the garden or the sky in a wild Yorkshire storm, for example.

QUICK FIX:
Feel your feelings

Use this tip to release pent-up emotion.

- Find a quiet space, either alone or with someone you can be yourself with.

- Close your eyes and take a few deep, slow breaths.

- Focus your mind on your emotional state for about one minute; notice the sensations in your body.

- Let yourself express these for 20 seconds or so – allow tears of sadness and disappointment to well up; let out a growl of anger; shudder out your fear.

- Take another three deep, slow breaths while mentally focusing on the passage of your breath.

- Have a comfort experience: if you are with someone, share your feelings and take any comfort offered (but don't get into further discussion which could unbalance you emotionally); if you are alone, give yourself a small, comforting treat.

SURROUND
YOURSELF
WITH STIRRING
SYMBOLS

. . . .

During the recession, my husband was becoming very
stressed by the pressure he was under from major clients to
make cuts in his prices that his business could not afford.
Not surprisingly, my verbal reminders about how important
it was to stay cool and assertive and not bow to unfair
pressure were falling on very deaf ears. So instead, I bought
him a very cute and delicately carved ancient mini Chinese
tiger. I suggested that he keep it hidden in a pocket of his
suit as a symbolic reminder of his need to stay calm and
strong in the face of economic bullying. He was amused
and used it. Now that he is back on his usual assertive
track, the little tiger sits in my consultation room and is
there to help anyone who needs a similar reminder.

Symbols are powerful motivators. They can communicate
an inspirational message at high speed and with emotional

impact. They can say in seconds something that might take many minutes or even hours to convey with words. So they are particularly useful when time is short, or concentration for reading or listening is elusive. And isn't this so often the case when you are battling through difficult patches in your life?

You could, of course, choose to use one of the many well-known archetypal symbols, such as a horse for power or a dove for peace. But for personal inspiration it is better to think of your own, as it will have much more emotional power for you.

Here are some very different examples that have helped others and which I hope will inspire you to think of one you could use:

- **A pressed sunflower** – to recall a simple happy holiday in a French cottage to help get some perspective when Jane was worrying about money.

- **Grandmother's brooch** – a reminder for Charlie of his grandmother's resilience in the face of extreme hardship and uncertainty during the war.

- **A mouse mat from Robben Island** where Nelson Mandela was imprisoned – a reminder of how people can learn how to give up aggression and switch to negotiation and diplomacy to effect change (one of my own!).

- Photo of the presentation to Peter's son of a Duke of Edinburgh award for charity work – used to remind Peter of his son's great qualities a few years later when he was on remand for drug-related crimes.

- Certificate of final school exams – a reminder to Paula that she had the intellectual capacity to pass the resit of her university exam.

If you leave your symbols around in the background of your life, they will be repeatedly absorbed into your subconscious mind along with the good feeling they trigger. It is also a good idea to keep your symbols in public view whenever you can. People are then likely to comment on them, and each time this happens, even if you don't choose to explain its personal significance, you will be reminded of it and receive an internal uplift. It could also give you an opportunity to share your goal or dream with more people who will probably become additions to your supportive team of encouragers.

QUICK FIX:
Transform possibilities into inspirational goals

Do you ever hear yourself starting a sentence with, "I suppose I could go/do/ask..." or, "One day, I might be able/try..." or, "I have thought of doing/saying/saving for..."?

From now on, whenever you catch yourself using one of these phrases, try to rephrase what you're saying. See if you can transform your possibility into a goal. Smile as you speak, and make a statement of intent by filling in the gaps in this sentence: "No, I am going to rephrase that. On [date] I will [action] and then I will reward myself by [treat]."

As soon as you can, commit your "action plan" to paper or make a note of it electronically. Then share your intention with as many of your friends, colleagues and acquaintances as you can. The more people who know of your intention, the higher your chances of staying on course and achieving success. I have found that many people leave off the treat at the end. Try not to do that though, as planning a reward for yourself will increase your motivation, as well as giving you an additional morale boost.

GET GROWING SOMETHING

At 45, Adrian was diagnosed with a motor neurone disease and it appeared to be progressing quite rapidly. Not only would it affect his capacity to work as an electrical engineer, it also threatened his ability to enjoy his hobby – archery. From an early age Adrian had shown a talent for archery, had now become captain of his regional team and had started coaching a new team of wheelchair archers. Most of his social life revolved around this sport.

Although Adrian was determined to stay positive in the face of his daunting diagnosis, he was inwardly very fearful of the restrictions that this invasive disease would put on his life.

One day, over lunch at work, his wife, Fay, was sharing her concerns about him with a group of colleagues. They were a group of very caring and practical women and were quick to come up with loads of alternative interests and hobbies. But one idea shone out as having the most possible appeal to Adrian. One woman had been involved in a fund-raising event for an organisation called Thrive (thrive.org.uk), which she knew had been a great help to a friend who had developed multiple sclerosis. She explained that this small national charity used gardening to change the lives of disabled people.

Fay knew that Adrian might consider this as an option because only a month previously, when they were sitting in their untidy jungle of a garden, Adrian had said that it was a pity that in their busy lives the gardening always fell to the bottom of their priority lists.

Adrian did decide to contact Thrive. The local organiser happened to live quite near by, so he popped round to explain their work further. Needless to say, he took a great interest in Adrian's wheelchair archery project and the two men instantly became friends. One year on, with the help of a team from Thrive, Adrian's garden is now an oasis of flowering tranquillity and two of Thrive's wheelchair-bound members are learning archery. Adrian plans to stay involved with the archery club when his illness progresses, if only in an advisory capacity, but he now knows that he has another hobby that will be just as challenging and absorbing which he can move on to.

"To be happy for an hour, get drunk; to be happy for a year, fall in love; to be happy for life, take up gardening."

....

Chinese proverb

Thrive has completed a number of research studies which show that gardening can help people going through all sorts of difficult periods in their lives. Janet Caruso, who works for the organisation, explains: "Gardening can help you get back on top of things and restore the balance when it feels like your life is veering out of control. It helps you to feel happier, more confident and healthier." She gave the following reasons why it can be such a great morale booster and positive diversion for anyone who may be at a low time in their life:

- It is great physical exercise.

- You can work at your own pace and in small steps.

- You can learn new skills which might be useful in other areas of your life.

- It can provide a great opportunity to meet people.

- It can offer an opportunity for self-expression and a chance to explore your creativity.

- Nurturing growing things can literally give you a reason to get out of bed in the morning and the satisfaction of knowing that you have made it happen.

- If you are finding everyday life hard to cope with, gardening outside could even help you to take a first step out of the house.

Like Adrian and Fay, I have very little time in my life for gardening. But I do know that just dead-heading a few roses or pulling the dead leaves off my poor houseplants works as a calming and satisfying diversion. So even if you only have time and space to grow a box of cress or plant a pot of bulbs, try this nurturing therapy.

CREATE A TEN-MINUTE HIBERNATION HAVEN

··················

"I think all I need is a few weeks of peace and I'll be fine... then I will be able to cope and know what I need to do."

··················

Jane, recently deserted by her boyfriend and father of her two young children

Jane had been happily living with her boyfriend for nine years. Their children were aged two and a half and eighteen months when he proposed that they take the big leap and get married. In preparation, they decided to move into a new, larger flat. One Saturday afternoon, they went out looking at various properties. On their return, Jane's boyfriend told her that he had changed his mind and could not "go through with it". He gathered up his belongings, walked out and has not been back since.

Not surprisingly, when Jane came to see me months later, she was still unable to come to terms with this totally unanticipated and inexplicable change in her life. We couldn't even begin to plan her next step because she was overwhelmed by the stresses of her everyday life. She had become fixated on the idea of a holiday in isolation as her solution and, as is often the case, this was an impossible fantasy.

Do you, like Jane, often find yourself yearning for a means of escape from your here and now? This is a very natural and normal response to a shock or ongoing stress. Your mind is simply answering the physiological needs it is sensing. It is saying that your body and brain are exhausted. They are in serious need of a recharge.

It may be of some comfort to know that even if it were feasible, an escape holiday could well make matters worse. People who are "lucky" enough to get away from it all on a sun-soaked beach or at a tranquil spa often find that on their return they feel even more sad, powerless or depressed than before.

A more positive alternative is to feed regularly the needs at the root of your yearning, and one way to do this is by creating an accessible haven in your home or office – wherever your safe space is. This will allow you to take frequent mini-escapes in tranquillity which will cost you virtually nothing and take up very little of your precious problem-solving time. Regular ten-minute recharges in your haven will give you a much-needed energy boost in the short term, while in the long term, they will prevent a toxic build-up of the side effects of the stress hormones that render you more vulnerable to all manner of disease and infection.

NO ROOM FOR EXCUSES!

You may well be saying or thinking: "Nice idea … if only it were possible!" And this was Jane's first response, followed by a series of other "excuses", before she finally agreed to have a go. So before we look at the practicalities of creating a haven, let's first deal with a few of the most common responses.

"There's no room or money for such a place"

Of course, ideally it would be wonderful to have a separate, sound-proofed room designed and equipped as a relaxation haven in every home and workplace. Such places do exist; I have seen and envied them. But they are a luxury that only a very privileged few can ever have, while the rest of us must create our haven within a room that serves many other purposes. This may initially require a little more imagination than a purpose-built haven, but the end result can be equally restorative.

"I'm far too busy and tired to take on anything else"

Saying this is a sure sign that you need an easy-to-use haven! You are at risk of both physical and mental ill health which would put even more pressure on your agenda and your body. Regular relaxation breaks in a very handy location are exactly what you need to keep your body and mind working well enough to support you through tough periods.

"I can't suddenly take over a space that belongs to others as well"

Of course you will need to negotiate with anyone else who has a right to use the space in question. But is that impossible? You would only need to use the haven area for periods of 10 minutes if it is well equipped and you become skilled at relaxation. Maybe others might join you when they witness the beneficial effect it has on you!

"Even if I had such a place I'd never use it . . . that's me"

You must believe that you can change. Certainly, your genetic inherited temperament and your past have shaped the personality traits you have today. But, by adopting new behavioural habits, you can both feel a different person and appear to be so to others. There is increasing evidence from recent neuroscience research which shows that if changes in behaviour are repeated frequently, new neural connections are created in the brain. This means that a "new you" could become a physical reality. So if you want to be the kind of person who "chills out" regularly, you can be.

HOW TO CREATE
AND USE YOUR
HAVEN

Let's assume that you do not have a spare room that could
be used solely as your haven – a room that is used quite
infrequently, perhaps for meetings or guests is an ideal
alternative – with the help of a free-standing screen, one
corner of a bedroom, sitting room or office can be left fully
prepared for use as your haven. Or, if this too is impossible,
with just a few simple props you can easily and quickly
create a good-enough ambience in any room. And your
props can be kept together in a small box, bag or chest that
can travel with you wherever you go.

When choosing the equipment for your haven, focus on
objects and furnishings that stimulate your senses rather
than your intellect. **Here is a list of some of the basics that
you may want to include:**

- **Comfortable seating:** the kind that allows you to lie with
  your back and neck supported and your feet up is ideal,
  but any chair will do with the help of a small back cushion
  (or rolled-up towel) and stool or other object on which to
  rest your legs.

- **Headphones:** preferably the noise-reduction kind that block out most external sounds.

- **Portable music player:** preloaded with music or sounds you find relaxing.

- **Low lighting:** a candle is ideal as the flicker of a flame is hypnotic. If you cannot dim the lights, have an eye mask to hand for some of the time. (Dim lighting stimulates the production of the hormone melatonin which helps to relax you in preparation for sleep.)

- **Relaxing and uplifting colours:** ensure that your favourite choice of both is in the furnishing or objects around you.

- **Scent:** choose ones which you associate with pleasure and relaxation, using room sprays, incense sticks, candles or burning oils or real scented flowers.

- **A few books containing pictures or photographs that have a soothing and pleasurable effect on you.** You could compile a special one with your own photos and postcards.

- **An alarm clock,** timer or stopwatch to ensure that you keep to your 10 minutes. If, for example, you should fall asleep and miss an important deadline, that would defeat the object of the exercise and you may never use your haven again.

TEN-MINUTE PROGRAMME FOR A HAVEN BREAK

1. **For 1 minute:** release tension from any taut muscles with some simple stretching exercises. Then, screw up your face, squeezing your eyes shut and letting out a big whoosh of breath when you release your muscles. Repeat a couple of times.

2. **For 4 minutes:** put on your headphones (with silence, music or sounds as you prefer), lie down or lounge and browse through one of your chosen books.

3. **For 4 minutes:** close your eyes or put on an eye mask; take three slow, deep breaths and allow yourself to sink into a physically and mentally relaxed state. You should feel as though you are a floating zombie!

4. **For 1 minute:** do a few stretches, then briskly march on the spot to re-energise your system.

QUICK FIX:
Cuddle yourself with comfy clothes

"When I free my body from its clothes, from all their buttons, belts and laces, it seems to me that my soul takes a deeper, freer breath."

August Strindberg, playwright

If you are someone who feels more at ease in pyjamas or other comfy clothes, why not apply this principle more liberally during tough times? Take a look at your wardrobe and view each garment in relation to its therapeutic qualities. Give each one a rating to reflect how good it is at helping you to feel relaxed or bringing a smile to your face through putting it on.

Most people find that their older outfits get the highest scores. So it should cost you precisely nothing to cuddle yourself more often in comfort clothing. Take a break from fashion and image slavery, and if you're worried about what others might think, remember the following wise words from fashion writer Lee Mildon: "People seldom notice old clothes if you wear a big smile."

RELATIONSHIPS

Your circle of support could, at different points, include family members, people from your social network, neighbours, work colleagues or just kind-hearted acquaintances from within your community. During difficult times, however, it is those people whom you regard as "friends" on whom you will probably depend the most. They are the people with whom you have an emotional bond, and there is an understanding (often unspoken) that you will give each other support. Of course, such friends may also play a dual role in that they are also family members, colleagues or your next-door neighbour – they might even share your bed if you are lucky enough to count on your partner as a friend.

When it comes to getting quality support it helps to know exactly who these friends are, and how they might be able to help you. In normal day-to-day life, you don't have to think too much about your friendships; you can afford to just let them wax and wane, as new faces appear in your life and others are left behind. But in difficult times, you may find that your "hotchpotch" circle of friends cannot provide you with the kind of support that you need. Even your very best and most willing friends have personality limitations, as well as restraints on their emotional reserves and possibly their time.

With this in mind, this section offers you tips that will help you to analyse your current circle of support and identify its strengths and weaknesses and show you ways in which you can extend and fortify it. Not all relationships are positive and the latter half of this section also shows you how to stand up to your critics and saboteurs and reclaim your sense of self-worth in the process.

QUICK FIX:
Feast with friends

"Eating or drinking without a friend is the life of a lion or a wolf"

Epicurus, philosopher

Anthropologists think that the very first social activity that primitive man created was that of sharing a meal. Ever since then, in every corner of the globe, coming together over food has been used to create and cement friendships.

At this moment in time, you may be too busy, tired, sad or broke to cook for your friends, so arranging the kind of feast to which everyone brings a dish could be the answer. I always find that there is delicious food at these events, because people usually bring along their best dish. Also, it gives people the option not to cook unless they want to do so. If you offer to host the occasion, you can provide the water, tea and coffee so you won't need to cook anything.

DRAW YOUR SUPPORT FROM YOUR FRIENDS' SPECIAL STRENGTHS

....

"A friend in need is a friend indeed."

....
English proverb

Friends can be drawn from your family, your social circle and your colleagues. If you appreciate each person's special strengths and draw mainly on these you will receive much better support from them. This will also reduce the chances of being disappointed by some of your friends and losing out on the other benefits those friendships can bring.

The exercise omn pages 44–51 will help you to appraise the special strengths of each of your friends, after which you will be able to draw on support from them more efficiently and quickly.

I often find people are reluctant to do this exercise – they say it sounds like an overly calculating approach to friendship. I agree that it may feel a bit odd to "categorise" the qualities of your friends because this is not something you would usually do formally (even though most of us do it informally through gossip, all the time). But it is now accepted practice to analyse personal strengths and aptitudes in the business world when assessing and selecting staff and collaborators to do a job, and also in the dating world when searching for a suitable partner. We do it in these fields because this kind of analysis works, so why not apply it to friendship too?

You should find that the exercise will also help you to give others better support. It raises your awareness of your own strengths and limitations in relation to friendship.

You will see that I have listed sixteen categories of friends on the following pages; each has a title that reflects their special strength in relation to a support role that you may need. Some friends will obviously be able to play a number of these roles quite adequately; but remember, some roles could possibly be played just as well or even more skilfully by someone else. It is always a good idea to see if you can "spread the load" before asking for the support you need. Even your very best or most caring friend has their limitations. This is why I suggest that you "nominate" at least one person as a back-up for the roles which you think you would need the most.

The exercise on the following page may reveal some gaps in your friendship circle, but don't panic, this will free you out to go and connect with new and wonderful people to enrich your life.

FRIENDSHIP ROLES: CHECKLIST EXERCISE

Look at the following list of sixteen roles that friends can play in order to offer support. Read it through first without making any mental or written notes. If you want to add one or more roles, feel free to do so. Next, list the roles on a piece of paper or on your computer. Think about each one more carefully now in relation to the friends you have and note down their names beside any of the roles that they do or could fulfil for you.

1. *The cheerful chatterers*

They have a sunny disposition. You can always count on them to be smiling and they are never lost for words. Their conversation is light and often predictable. They don't need explanations for everything and tend to take life as it comes. They are relaxing and easy to be with.

2. *The old timers*

They share a good deal of history with you and love to look back at the old days. They help you to remember the young you and the you who has survived life's ups and downs.

Conversation with them brings you a "Mum's cooking" kind of glow that is comforting and boosts your self-esteem.

3. The adventurers

They always have something new and interesting to tell you about their lives. They encourage you out of your comfort zone, and get you excited about doing something new.

4. The caring listeners

They will listen to you with genuine interest and without interruptions. You feel better after talking to them, even though you may be no nearer a solution.

5. The devil's advocates

These are the friends who always seem to come up with an opposite point of view. They may do this just because they get a kick out of arguing and debating. This can be useful because they can help you to understand others better, especially when your feelings are intense and could be blinding you in some way. Also, your arguments with them can help you to firm up your views and decisions and make you more determined and able to put forward your ideas or case more convincingly.

6. The clowns

You can always count on them to see the funny side of a black situation. Having a laugh with them is very relaxing and sometimes enlightening. They can also be great for taking you down a peg or two if you have become a bit blinded to your own faults and limitations.

7. The thinkers

These are very sensible friends. They are especially good to talk to when a situation is complicated or emotionally charged. They will help you to weigh up the pros and cons before taking any action. This can save you acting hastily and repenting later. These friends are also good to talk to when you'd like to take your mind off your problems for a while. They love discussions which involve finding solutions to any kind of issue or problem. Talking with them is like doing a workout on your mind; it will distract you from your problems, while at the same time making your mental muscles stronger.

8. The doers

These are not the best listeners in the world, but if you
need some practical help you can count on them to get
cracking without delay. They often need some guidance
from you about what needs doing as they are doers rather
than thinkers, but they usually get a great buzz out of being
needed, so don't hold back from asking.

9. The SOS rescuers

These are your truly "cool" friends, in that they keep their
heads in a crisis. Indeed, they are often at their best during
tough times. Even if they are not very practical themselves,
you can count on them to have a list of useful contacts.

10. The soldiers

These friends will stand up for you when you may not
be capable of fighting your own corner. They are super-
assertive, and even prepared to be aggressive when they
see a great injustice being done. They have good stamina
and persistence, so you can count on them to be around for
longer than others. They are also good at getting an "army"
of support together from their own contacts to give you
even more back-up.

11. *The financiers*

These friends are great budgeters and always know where the bargains and good deals can be found. They are great if you need some extra money. Some may be more than happy to help out with some extra no-strings-attached money. Others may be able to offer "safe" advice on loans that will not burden you with a debt you cannot truly afford.

12. *The visionaries*

These are great people with whom to talk through your dreams and hopes. They will often encourage you to think "big" and take a long-term perspective. This means that they are very good people to take to lunch if you are obsessing about too many of today's little problems or have been stuck in the same rut for too long.

13. *The inspirational survivors*

These friends don't need to *do* anything in particular to help you. They have already done their bit by having faced and come through difficult challenges. Their strength is that they are a living example to you of how you could become stronger (and even nicer!) as a result of tough times. So in order to give you support they just need to be themselves and be a presence in your life. Simply talking about the weather with them can remind you of their inspirational story and be enough to give you a boost of courage and confidence.

14. *The competitive companions*

These people make goal-getting fun. They are always willing to challenge you to have a go against them. You don't have to worry about damaging their confidence as they are great losers as well as winners. Competing with them in any kind of way will help you to extend your potential and so increase your confidence.

15. *The people-readers*

These are the friends who not only read other people's minds but yours too! They can be very good at seeing through your self-defensive waffle, even when you can't. They can help you to understand why people may have acted in a certain way or said things which puzzle or enrage you. Also, if they are people you know you can trust, you can have some satisfying character assassination sessions with them! This can help you to let off steam after you have had to take some stick from people who have upset or bullied you.

16. The soulmates

These are often referred to as "best" friends. They know
and understand you so well that you may not even need
to speak before they know what's bothering you. You
can count on their love for you whatever and whenever.
Even though you may not have seen them for ages, your
relationship slots back into the same place as soon as you
meet again. You can always be yourself with them and know
that your secrets and disclosures are safe. But, however
special these friends are, they can never fulfil all the above
roles; and, in times of crisis, they may be too shocked or
emotional on your behalf to even be able to fulfil those they
normally do well.

Now that you've worked through the list, can you identify
any gaps? Perhaps you have lots of friends who are fun
and social, but none that can be relied on to be practical
and calm in a crisis. Once you have identifed these gaps,
try to make new connections to fortify and strengthen
your friendship groups. It may be that one of your existing
friends is more practical than you realise, but you've never
explored that side of their personality, or perhaps it's time
to widen your circle of friends and let some new people in.
You can never have too many friends, afterall.

So in these difficult days, forget worrying about who is a "true" friend and who isn't. Some friends may happen to have more to offer you at this point, while others may come into their own at another time. And remember, the support that a friend can give you in your hour of need is not necessarily a reflection of how good that person is or is not. Nor is it an indication of the degree of love they have for you. Sometimes, your nearest and dearest are useless in a crisis and it can be the neighbour you hardly speak to who becomes your star support.

QUICK FIX:
Deepen your key relationships

> **"Soulmates are people who bring out the best in you. They are not perfect, but are always perfect for you."**
>
> Anonymous

Research has shown that you can instantly deepen your relationships with people you care most about by increasing any one of the following five factors (but why not go for the whole package as soon as you can?):

1. Time **2.** Touch **3.** Sharing **4.** Caring **5.** Fun

As a mum whose daughter is on the other side of the world, I can't instantly increase the "touch" factor, but I have found video calling is a very satisfying second best. And, if you're as soppy as I am, you can always touch the screen!

Strengthening your soulmate relationships should always be a high priority. These people may not be able to fulfil many of the support roles you need right now, but you can count on them to be at your side come rain or shine.

*"When it hurts to look back,
and you're scared to look ahead,
you can look beside you and your
best friend will be there."*

Anonymous

BACK OFF SENSITIVELY FROM MORALE-DRAINERS

....

"A true friend knows your weaknesses but shows you your strengths; feels your fears but fortifies your faith; sees your anxieties but frees your spirit; recognises your disabilities but emphasises your possibilities."

....

William Arthur Ward, writer

This sums up very well the qualities of morale-boosting friends. Morale-drainers are their direct opposites. At best, they are overly self-focused, will more or less ignore you, or take you for granted; while at worst, they may know your strengths, but remind you constantly of your weaknesses;

they can be insensitive about your fears, disappointments and sadness and they may be disrespectful about your beliefs. When you are with them or have just left them, you can sense that your hope and self-confidence are deflated. And, to make matters worse, you usually also feel physically tired and too apathetic around them to do anything, let alone rise to your own defence!

First rule: let yourself off the hook. Because you are going through a rough patch yourself, this is not the time to either confront them or feel sorry for them.

The second rule is to back off as fast as you can. A few white lies to use as excuses are, in my opinion, quite justified. But make sure they are ones where you won't be caught out. The best advice I can give here is to provide them with the minimum of information.

So when they are talking and you feel you need to back off, you can say briefly and quickly: "Sorry to interrupt, but I have a dinner date. I must go immediately. Take care and have a good evening. Bye." Don't get involved with long explanations, such as: "I'm very sorry to interrupt. It is not that I don't want to listen; it's just that I'm meeting Margaret in a minute – we are having dinner. She is having a hard time since her husband had that affair and

I really mustn't be late. So sorry to have to break off our conversation. But you know me; I'm always in a rush. We'll catch up again next week, perhaps. You know where I am if you need me."

The latter gives the morale-drainer lots of unnecessary information which can prompt questions. It also is over-apologetic and even includes a self-put-down, ending with an attempt to soften the blow by inviting another date for a catch-up. All these are common mistakes. At first, you may feel it is rude to be brief. But it's not; it is simply being assertive and setting boundaries.

An alternative, super-assertive way of handling this situation is to be even more direct and say something like: "Sorry, I'm finding it hard to concentrate. I'm switching off because I don't want to get depressed. I have to look after number one right now. It would be best if you could find someone else to talk to about this. I hope you will under-stand that I have to say goodbye now. Take care."

But don't forget – the first example I gave is good enough. Don't you have a right to protect yourself from morale-drainers? It's to no one's advantage to have yet another depressed person in the world!

STANDING UP
TO SABOTAGE
....

It is amazing to me how, in very difficult problem situations, even truly nice people can become critical, arrogant, know-alls and interfering busy-bodies. Often, their intentions are well meaning, but their interference and advice are not helpful. This could be because you are not ready to take the action they suggest, or you want to try doing it in your own way.

I admit that I too can become one of those people, when someone I care about deeply is in distress. My horrible, bossy side takes over from my nurturing one. Luckily, my family are assertive enough to tell me to back off, but less confident friends will unfortunately tend to just go quiet on me. With a few sad exceptions, I can now spot this happening. But this wasn't always the case. Before going through many years of personal and professional development training, I didn't have enough self-awareness and sensitivity to spot emotional clues from others to stop this sabotaging behaviour from damaging relationships.

Perhaps you have already encountered this kind of annoying hindrance from others. If so, I hope you have managed to give them the 'back-off' message. But if you find that difficult to do, you may first need to firm up your belief in your rights to do this.

The exercise opposite will help you to fix your personal rights in your memory, after which you should find that when you encounter sabotaging behaviour, one or more of these rights will instantly spring into your mind. Some people say that it is like having a guardian angel (or me!) sitting on their shoulder, reminding them to stand up for themselves.

HOW TO DEAL
WITH SABOTEURS

- Read through the list below and tick those rights that relate most to you and your situation. Make a note in your mind or on paper of how they can be disrespected in your everyday life; remember that people can be disrespectful of your rights even though they may be motivated by the very best intentions (the "I-was-only- trying-to-help" syndrome).

- Personalise this list of rights by adapting, adding or subtracting rights.

- Write down your own personal rights list and read it out loud at least once every day for a week.

✓ **I have the right to do things my way.**

✓ **I have the right to make my own decisions and cope with the consequences.**

✓ **I have a right to make mistakes.**

✓ **I have a right to not be a perfect person.**

✓ **I have a right to privacy.**

✓ **I have a right not to know about or understand something.**

✓   I have a right to change my mind.

✓   I have a right to be alone sometimes

✓   I have a right to take some time to heal and recover

✓   I have a right to feel what I feel

✓   I have a right to refuse help that I don't think I need

✓   I have a right to be treated as an individual

✓   I have a right to ask for help, even though I may be refused

✓   I have a right to choose who I want to be with

✓   I have a right to move at my own pace

✓   I have a right to be positive and optimistic

✓   I have a right to seek professional help if I choose

✓   I have a right to read self help books!

Once you have firmly established these rights in your mind, you will be able to make good use of the rest of the tips in this section.

SAY "NO" AS THOUGH YOU MEAN IT
. . . .

When your morale is low, your ability to communicate in an assertive manner is almost always affected, so that you may often find yourself more open to being led into doing things that you would prefer not to do. Until you are feeling emotionally stronger, use these tips to help your "No" to come across more powerfully:

- As soon as you hear the question or suggestion, move deliberately into a confident pose by placing both feet on the ground and straightening your posture.

- Use the trick of pausing before saying something important. In this moment, concentrate on taking at least one slower and deeper breath. This will help to deepen your voice and keep it steady.

- Catch the eye of the person before starting to speak. Or you can look at their ear if you can't face direct eye contact – it has the same effect!

- Don't give reasons for your refusal; they provide ammunition for an argument for which you probably haven't enough energy or confidence to win, so just stick with a short, direct polite statement such as: "No, I would prefer not to do that today. But thank you for asking."

- If they try and persuade you with a seductive plea, just repeat the same statement, including an emphatic word and leaving out the thanks. Trust that the repetition is very important, even though it may sound parrot-like to you at first: "No, I really would prefer not to do that today."

- If they ask you what you are doing instead, don't tell them. That again would offer them "food" to argue that what they are suggesting would be better. Simply say: "It's nothing to do with anything I am doing, it's just that I don't want to do that today." By this time, they should have got the message – if not, just persist with your repetition until they do, and they will!

QUESTION YOUR CRITICS TO MAKE THEM CONSTRUCTIVE

....

"Criticism may not be agreeable, but it is necessary. It fulfils the same function as pain in the human body. It calls attention to an unhealthy state of things."

....

Winston Churchill, British Prime Minister (1940–45 and 1951–55)

Instead of clamming up when criticism hits, empower yourself by calmly and confidently asking information-seeking questions. If your critic is capable of being constructive, this will usually bring forth some good suggestions. If your critic can't come up with an answer because, perhaps, they are in a bad mood and you were an easy target, this kind of questioning takes them aback. You will then find you have effectively stopped them in their critical tracks. So whatever their response, you are a winner.

Unless you have tried this kind of tactic before, it may seem very hard to do. But actually it just takes practice. Watch confident people use it, such as politicians when they are dealing with aggressive interviewers. They have probably been trained in this technique.

It is easy to train yourself and can be good fun to practise it with a friend. They can play the role of someone who you think really would like to take you down a peg or two. Even if you never get the opportunity to do this in real life, you will have had a good morale boost from just doing the rehearsal.

"We don't criticise. Criticism is an enemy. You've got to make loving, positive suggestions."

....

Dorothy Sarnoff, singer and pioneer of self-help

QUESTIONS TO
USE WITH CRITICS

When dealing with critics, it can be easy to let self-doubt take over and accept the negativity that is being directed at you without question. Instead, try and bring their accusations into focus by asking for more detail. This will either help the criticism become constructive or expose unjust treatment if they are unable to back up their initial statements. As a starting point, try the questions below:

1. Request specific details if they are generalising

- "How many times have you noticed that I?"

- "What do you actually hear me say or do?"

2. Request clarification if they are hinting

- "Are you saying that I'm not capable of working yet?"

- "Do you mean to say that I am lazy?"

- "Do you think I am a hysteric and not really that heart-broken?"

3. Request more criticism

- "Is there anything else you think I am doing wrong or could do better?"

- "Is there anything else about my character that you don't like or irritates you?"

QUICK FIX:
Call in your army if the going gets too tough

Very often, setbacks require that you take on battles with dauntingly large organisations (such as social security systems or insurance companies with one-size-fits-all rules) or imposing authority figures (such as your child's opinionated head teacher when they've just failed their exams).

In these situations, or any others where you might be up against a first-class bully, don't hesitate to rally support. Bullying tactics require group force to out-manoeuvre them at the best of times.

Remember the friends you labelled "the soldiers" on p.47? They are the people to call on now. Perhaps if these weren't such hard times for you, you could manage on your own. But why not give yourself a break and use the extra support?

FINANCES

I would guess that many of you will have some kind of money worries weighing on your mind, simply because so many setbacks have either direct or indirect implications on financial resources. Even if your main source of income is not directly threatened, the cost of dealing with your problems may be worryingly high fees for lawyers, estate agents, medical practitioners or undertakers, for example. Or you may need extra smaller sums to cover increased travel, takeaway meals, stationery and books for information. And in the heat of a problem situation, people often (understandably) spend less discriminately, so that debts accrue more rapidly.

When you feel helpless like this, your morale and mood can sink to their lowest depths. Research undertaken by a charity in the UK called The FairBanking Foundation (fairbanking.org.uk) has revealed that there is a strong correlation between wellbeing and the extent to which you have control over your finances. And this is exactly why I've included this short section on the subject, with expert input from The FairBanking Foundation's founder, Antony Elliott.

The tips here may not solve the major problems that are at the root of your worries, but they will boost your morale because you will feel more in control of some important aspects of your financial health. This section also has some ideas that could help you to make some real savings. You could then afford little treats to keep you motivated or maybe some extra help with services that might lessen the drain on your time and energy.

KEEP FEELINGS AND FINANCES APART

Emotional decision-making (i.e. responding according to the guidance from your "gut feelings") may work well in some areas of your life, but it should never be allowed to take any control in the management of your finances. This is especially so during difficult times when your emotional temperature is running hot and there is a danger that your feelings will get the better of you.

Your fear, for example, could make you too risk-averse and this might cause you to overly restrict your spending and suffer unnecessary inconvenience and insufficient uplifting treats. Or, on the other hand, your emotional state could lead you into doing just the opposite with even worse consequences. You're bound to have heard someone who was going through a rough patch say something like the following; or maybe even have said it yourself: "What the hell – in for a penny, in for a pound; things can't get any worse, so what does it matter? I know it's a lot of money, but let's go for it."

If you are in the position of needing the comfort of some financial cushioning, or you need to acquire extra resources, make sure that you defuse your feelings before doing any financial planning or decision-making.

"The emotional brain doesn't just understand things like interest rates or debt payments or finance charges."

....

Jonah Lehrer, author of *The Decisive Moment – How the Brain Makes Up Its Mind*

HAVE THREE PERSONAL BUDGETS INSTEAD OF ONE

Let's assume you do already have a current budget for your personal finances as they stand now. This means that you will only need to create an extra two. Unless your financial situation changes dramatically (for the worse or for the better), you may never actually need to use either of the budgets I suggest you now draw up. The purpose of doing them is purely psychological.

Your second budget, the "survival budget", will help you to contain your financial fears, while the third, the "hopeful budget", should give you an injection of optimism. It will remind you that things could improve financially for you even though you may find this difficult to believe right now. After all, none of us can be totally sure which way our fortunes may travel.

THE SURVIVAL BUDGET

This should be a worst-case scenario forecast. It is particularly important to do if your income and savings are in danger of being drastically reduced as a result of your difficulties. It will help you to ease your worries.

So for each essential expense heading in your budget, put in a figure that is the minimum amount of money that you would require in order to meet that need without harming your own health or your family's (if you are supporting them). You should find the grand total is reassuring; it usually is for most people. If it is not, and if it scares you, start a "rainy-day" savings plan straight away. I have been through many financially frightening times and am always surprised and delighted by how useful sums of money can be accumulated through simple ideas, such as having savings jars for different kinds of coin.

Just before the current global financial crisis hit, my husband and I had started planning a special holiday, but on learning that my pension would now be drastically depleted, I felt panic. To cheer myself up, I bought a cheap savings box in the shape of a fat cow. The cow now sits on

the worktop in our kitchen and my husband and I goad
each other into "feeding" her from time to time. Of course,
our cash cow's real value is not monetary but psychological.
She serves as a humorous reminder to keep a sense of
perspective. After all, even if we end up camping we will
still have our holiday.

THE HOPEFUL BUDGET

This is the best-case scenario. Imagine that you are going
to have a substantial increase in your income. Now, for
each non-essential category, increase the amount you have
allocated in your current budget. Make sure that you add
in an amount for some motivating luxury treats for rewards
and celebrations. Then read my next tip! It may help you
acquire some of these, even if your circumstances stay
much the same for a while.

BORROW DON'T BUY

Before using this tip, you will need to edit out any negative
messages about borrowing that are circling around on your
hard drive. In the UK culture that I was brought up in we

received many strong directives against both borrowing and lending, summed up by the proverb, "Who goes a borrowing, goes a sorrowing", and Shakespeare's much-quoted, "Never a borrower or a lender be". In fact, it today's world where the importance or reducing waste and living sustainably is becoming ever more prevalent, borrowing, rather than buying, is becoming an increasing necessity.

Of course, neither lenders nor borrowers should engage with people they mistrust, and they should be aware that there is a slight risk involved in this kind of transaction. But I am suggesting that, in the main, you borrow goods and appliances more freely from friends and neighbours. As long as you know you can – and will – return what has been loaned, and you are fully prepared to be a lender too, there are many advantages to be had from being braver about borrowing. And during hard times the argument is even stronger. Here are some reasons why:

- **You offer people an easy way to help you. I believe that the vast majority of people do want to help others who have problems. They may not offer help because they don't want to interfere or embarrass you, or they may simply be too shy or too busy to notice you need help. My experience is, however, that when you do ask people if they could lend you something you need, they are only too willing, and even appear to get pleasure from helping.**

- By asking to borrow, you make it much easier for others to ask a favour from you. So you are likely to encounter another self-esteem-building opportunity.

- Although borrowing when you are in need can sometimes feel a little humbling, it can be positive in that it keeps your feet on the ground by reminding you that you do need some interdependence with others.

- When two people enter into a borrowing-lending "contract", trust between them must come into play. This brings people closer together and usually they become more mutually supportive.

- It makes financial sense to borrow rather than buy something you would rarely use.

- It is more ecologically sound to share the use of something that costs the environment to produce.

- If you are still nervous about asking to borrow, here are three tips to make it easier:

- Give the lender an easy escape route, by saying something like: 'Please feel free to say no; I am sure that I can ask someone else.' Or, 'I can manage fine without it, but I thought I would ask in case you could lend it to me. It would just make it easier to/be quicker than . . . '

- Specify the time when you will return or pay for what you have borrowed.

- Indicate your willingness to lend in return by saying something like, "Of course, if there is ever anything you need or want to borrow, please don't hesitate to ask me."

Here are a few suggestions of things you could borrow to save you money and strengthen your friendships and relationships with neighbours:

- **Books:** make a list for your friends and colleagues of those you have to lend and ask others to do the same. Or invite your neighbours for coffee and a mutual browse at books for borrowing.

- **Tools and occasional furniture:** many of these are used very irregularly, such as long ladders, paint-strippers, spare tables and chairs, put-me-up beds and power hoses.

- **Clothes:** especially those expensive outfits that you may only use for one-off occasions; most people are flattered by this kind of request.

- **Baby equipment:** I recall very happily lending my crib out seventeen times in the three years before I needed it again myself.

- **A home for a holiday:** nowadays, most people and families have contacts scattered around the world. You could suggest a home exchange that would give both parties an interesting weekend or holiday break. Or, if you know someone with a second home, they may be willing to have friends stay there – this is a good way for the property to be checked and aired and usually it strengthens contact with the neighbours.

- **Cars:** some people have second cars sitting around doing very little, or they may not use their car during the week. You may be willing to come to a borrowing arrangement that includes an attractive 'share-the- expenses' deal for them, but would still save you lots of money. Alternatively, you could consider the setting up of a neighbourhood or company car pool. Or you could suggest an exchange of lifts to the supermarket or school to save on petrol.

"One of the best ways to do yourself a favour is to lend somebody else a helping hand."

....

Anonymous

QUICK FIX:
Swap services to save and give support

Think of services you could offer to your friends, neighbours and colleagues. This could be a professional skill, such as fixing leaks if you are a plumber, for example, or a personal talent, such as making delicious, nutritious soups if you cook well. Distribute the list of services which you can offer, together with a brief note about why you want to start a swap-services scheme. Wait and see what happens. It'll cost you nothing but an hour of your time, and it could save you and your friends a considerable sum of money.

PHYSICAL HEALTH

"HI GAEL – I'M ALL RIGHT, ALTHOUGH WORKING A LOT. BUT I HAVE UPPED MY PERSONAL TRAINER SESSIONS TO TWICE A WEEK! IT HAS MADE A DIFFERENCE – TO MY MOOD, ANYWAY!"

Email from a former client going through a difficult time

On receiving this message, I let out a sigh of relief; it reassured me that my client had turned a corner. She had rung me the previous month in a very upset state, having heard some disturbing news about her work situation. But this email told me that she was now doing what she needed to do in order to survive a tough period of high stress.

Stress has a major debilitating effect on the body, so you need to take extra care with your health in tough times. You will need all the energy you can muster, even if your problem does not require much actual physical activity. While I am not a professional expert in this field, I do know from painful experience the effects of not taking good enough physical care of yourself during diffi- cult times.

Most people under stress do the exact opposite of what my client did. They sideline their health maintenance routines, slacken off their exercise programmes and also often skip meals, eat unhealthy fast food and drink too much caffeine and alcohol. It is so important not to let this happen though. Doubling up on personal trainer time, as my client did, would probably be a mood-downer for me – and possibly for you too. Instead, I would increase my walks and stretching exercises in order to release my tension and get an extra supply of oxygen. But whatever health-care programme it is that works for you, be sure not to let it fall by the wayside. You need to take more, not less, care of your body during times of high stress.

This is why I've included this section with tips on basic care that have helped me and encouraged many others. So read on to find out what you can do to ensure your body gets the extra care it needs.

QUICK FIX: *Eat for energy and health 80 per cent of the time*

This is about achieving the right balance between sensible and sensual eating. Of course, most of the time you should eat food that keeps you physically healthy. But we are all often motivated to eat foods that satisfy not just our nutritional needs, but also our sensual ones. And it's often during difficult times that the urge for "comfort" eating kicks in.

This is why I suggest that you establish a percentage figure to help you. I recommend 80/20 as a guide for people with normal metabolism and no serious food disorders. This means that you take care to eat healthily and sensibly for approximately 80 per cent of the time. Then, for the remaining 20 per cent, you can allow yourself to eat for fun.

Note: extra care must be taken with non-sensible foods if you suffer with serious weight, diabetic or allergy issues.

MAKE FITNESS FUN

Everyone knows how essential exercise is for physical health. But not enough attention is given to its power to improve emotional and mental wellbeing. You need it to oxygenate your brain into action and release tension so you can relax. The aerobic kind which makes you puff and sweat will also produce a surge of endorphins which induce feelings of wellbeing and pleasure.

During difficult times, normal fitness routines are often sidelined. Worry, anxiety and sadness all deplete your energy, so your usual trip to the gym or run round the park requires too much effort. In these times, you may have to change or adapt your exercise routine so that it feels easier and more enticing.

First, think about what stimulates enjoyment in you – we are all different in this respect. Then you can match one or more of these stimulators with some kind of uplifting exercise that you will enjoy. **On the following page are a few examples to give you the idea:**

STIMULATOR	ACTIVITY
Adventure	Cycling or rambling with new friends to new places
Competition	Competitive sports
Challenge	Stretching goals, such as marathons; classes for new skills
Music	Dance; aqua-aerobics
Conversation	Rambling groups; ballroom dancing
Travel	Activity weekend breaks; cycling tours; river rowing
Animals	Walking dogs (you can borrow one!); horse-riding
Spiritual experiences	yoga
Intellectual stimulation	Exercising at home while listening to radio discussions, quizzes or documentaries

AIM FOR QUALITY SLEEP

. . . .

Peter and Rebecca's son Charlie is a sergeant in the British army. At a time when the war in Afghanistan had started to re-escalate and was dominating the headlines in all the media, Charlie was posted to the front line. Understandably, neither Peter nor Rebecca was sleeping well. Both were becoming so exhausted that their insomnia was affecting their work and also their relationship. They were irritable with each other and spending much less time having fun together. Neither would consider taking sleeping tablets; they wanted to remain alert through the night in case they received a call from the army.

Peter and Rebecca were right to be concerned and seek advice. Research shows that sleep fragmentation and deprivation can have a negative effect on the brain for weeks. We have known for a long time how crucial sleep is for memory, but new findings have shown that it also affects the ability to adjust to change and find new solutions.

I am sure that this isn't the news that you want to hear when you're going through tough times. The chances are that your normal sleep patterns have been disrupted and may well be for a long time, but what can you do about it?

I advised Peter and Rebecca to stop counting the hours of sleep they were getting. Instead, I suggested that they try and ensure that the sleep they did have was the very best quality it could be. This gave them something positive to do, which is always a good way to divert the mind from worries.

If you are finding that you are getting less sleep than you need, take a look at the checklist opposite. Try using it for a week or two – it really is vital that the hours of sleep that you do get are as restful and refreshing as they can be.

And last, but not least, don't forget:

"If you can't sleep, then get up and do something instead of lying there and worrying. It's the worry that gets you, not the loss of sleep."

....

Dale Carnegie, personal development guru

CONDITIONS THAT AID QUALITY SLEEP	HAVE YOU...
Tension-free muscles	done your stretches and/or had a warm bath?
Dark room	got an eyeshade by the bed; blackout lining behind curtains or blinds?
Low noise level	got your earplugs, in case?
Carbohydrate snack	eaten a nutritious small portion of cereal; rice or oat biscuit?
Calming drink	tried a camomile infusion; milk?
Caffeine-free system	made sure you haven't had coffee since lunchtime?
Low alcohol levels	had one rather than two glasses of wine or beer?
Comfortable temperature	got a fan/heater on/extra blanket to hand?
Mind at ease	written a to-do list and shelved it at least two hours ago?

QUICK FIX:
Snack at a snail's pace

The little-and-often rule is good to remember in times of stress. Slow yourself down by stopping after every few mouthfuls to become aware of colours, shapes and textures on your plate, as well as the different sensations of taste. This will calm your troubled nerves, while at the same time making things easier for your digestive system. Chewing slowly gives the enzymes in your saliva longer to do their digestive work – breaking down some of the chemical bonds that connect the simple sugars that comprise starches. Also, there are some glands under your tongue whose secretions work on the digestion of fat – so the more snacking you do at a snail's pace, the more chance they have to do their job efficiently.

Great energising snacks to have in your pocket or on your desk are ones that need lots of chewing, such as dried vegetables and fruit and nuts.

FEED A
POSITIVE
MOOD

· · · · · · · · · · · · ·

The UK Mental Health Foundation recommends boosting
your intake of certain nutrients to target common mood
problems, as follows:

PROBLEM	NUTRIENTS
Anxiety	Folic acid and magnesium
Poor concentration	Vitamin B1
Depression	Vitamins B3, B6 and C, folic acid, magnesium, selenium, zinc, omega 3 fatty acids, tryptophan, tyrosine and GABA
Irritability	Vitamin B6, magnesium, selenium

Work out the areas you need to boost from the table on the previous page, then find at least one or two key foods from the list below and add them to your shopping list!

Foods that will provide the required nutrients

NUTRIENT	FOOD
Folic acid	Green leafy vegetables, calf liver and turkey, cod, salmon, halibut, shrimp, sesame seeds, hazelnuts and cashew nuts, walnuts, most beans and pulses, oranges
Vitamin B1	Wholegrain/brown bread, oats, rice, barley, pasta, lentils, peppers, cabbage, broccoli, asparagus, lettuce, mushrooms, spinach, watercress, green peas, aubergine, sunflower seeds, Brazil nuts, hazelnuts, pecans, pine nuts, pistachios, sesame seeds, tuna, salmon, mussels, pork

NUTRIENT	FOOD
Vitamin B3	Brown rice, rice bran, wheatgerm, broccoli, mushrooms, cabbage, sprouts, courgette/zucchini, squash, peanuts, beef liver and kidneys, pork, turkey, chicken, tuna, salmon, sunflower seeds
Vitamin B6	Brown rice, oats, bran, barley, bananas, mango, tuna, trout, salmon, avocados, watercress, cauliflower, cabbage, peppers, squash, asparagus, pak choi/bok choy, potatoes, chicken, pork, turkey, lima beans, soya beans, chick peas, sunflower seeds
Vitamin C	Red peppers, red cabbage, broccoli, sprouts, cauliflower, strawberries, oranges, tangerines, kiwi, cranberries, pineapple

NUTRIENT	FOOD
Magnesium	Spinach, watercress, avocados, peppers, broccoli, green cabbage, almonds, Brazil nuts, cashews, peanuts, macadamias, walnuts, pecans, pumpkin, sunflower seeds, poppy seeds, oatmeal, buckwheat, barley, quinoa, plain yoghurt, baked beans, bananas, kiwi, blackberries, strawberries, oranges, raisins
Selenium	Wheat germ, brewer's yeast, calf liver, turkey breast, cod, tuna, halibut, salmon, shrimp, mushrooms, garlic, spinach, sunflower seeds, tofu, barley, rye, oats, brown long-grain rice, mozzarella cheese, mustard and sunflower seeds

In addition, drink more water, herbal and fruit infusions and pure fruit juices. Not drinking enough fluid has significant implications for mental health. During an average day in the UK, an adult's body loses approximately 2.5 litres of water through the lungs as water vapour, through the skin as perspiration or through the kidneys as urine. In times of stress you lose even more water than usual from your body. If sufficient fluids (the recommended minimum is 2 litres a day) are not consumed to replace this loss, the symptoms of inadequate hydration can appear, including increased irritability, loss of concentration and reduced efficiency in mental tasks.

QUICK FIX:
Write away your worries

"Worry does not empty tomorrow of its sorrow; it empties today of its strength."

Corrie ten Boom, campaigner and writer

Corrie ten Boom joined the Dutch underground movement during the Nazi occupation in the Second World War. When it was discovered that she was hiding Jews, she and her family were sent to prison and concentration camps. She survived only because she was released as a result of a clerical error. She spent much of the rest of her life writing and rehabilitating survivors of prison experiences all over the world.

A tried-and-tested way to deal with worries is to get them out of your head and on to paper. Keep a little book to jot them down in to hand. When choosing your book, try to find one that has pages which can be easily torn out. You can then do a monthly review and rip out the pages that are no longer a big issue for you. You will be surprised at how quickly your book disappears!

QUICK FIX:
Heed hunger pangs

Allowing yourself to become too hungry can make you irritable, eat too quickly and get indigestion, reach out for fast foods that are fattening and not very nutritional and eat much more than you need.

Avoid these unnecessary knocks to your self-esteem and physical wellbeing by heeding your hunger pangs at an early stage. Always have a nutritious snack to hand. You may need more of these because your normal meal schedule is likely to be interrupted in difficult times.

MENTAL
WELLBEING

No one is immune to having their self-confidence knocked a little at some time during a difficult period. Even when a setback is not due to any personal failure, the prospect of change can create an internal wobble of self-doubt and, at these times, the cacophony of internal voices be far harder to quell than any external factors.

This section focuses on transforming these internal critics into personal cheerleaders who we can always carry with us to boost our confidence in times of stress or worry. For those of you who may already have a good deal of confidence, these tips can just serve as a reminder – as in the heat of a challenge, the habit of continually nurturing confidence can slip. For others, however, they might prove to be a more fundamental eye-opener to confidence building.

Most of the tips in this section focus on feeding self-esteem. This lies at the heart of self-confidence and you need it in abundance when you are faced with big challenges. You cannot overdose on these tips; they will not make you arrogant or selfish. Neither will they infuse you with a false conviction that you can achieve absolutely anything you set your mind to. But they will give you a more positive belief in yourself than I imagine you may already have, and keep this vital certainty burning brightly, so that you have hope and confidence when you most need them.

This section also includes tips designed to extend your self-knowledge and keep your focus moving positively forward, preventing you from being too hard on yourself over any past failures or current weaknesses.

BE KINDER
TO YOUR
WEAKNESSES

....

*"Our strength grows out
of our weaknesses."*

....

Ralph Waldo Emerson,
American poet and essayist

When you are feeling low and anxious, your weaknesses
tend to leap to the forefront of your mind, and, as a result,
you may frequently find yourself blaming them for the
mess and stress in your life.

Gerry, a senior manager, had recently been made
redundant. At one level in his mind, Gerry knew that the
decision to cut his post had been purely made as part of a
cost-cutting exercise. But you'd find this difficult to believe
if you took his self-accusatory ramblings at face value:

"I don't know what it is about me. I was the oldest person in the office and I know that my age was against me fitting in. But this is not the first time my job has been axed. I thought I was doing reasonably OK this time, but perhaps I'm not cut out for top management. I'm too soft for my own good."

I have heard so many different variations on this kind of derogatory self-talk. There is of course a reason why this self-defeating habit sets in during difficult times. It is caused by that inevitable dip in self-esteem that accompanies problems that make us feel powerless. If you find yourself thinking or talking like this, you might find that logical reasoning alone does nothing to budge this habit. So the next time someone responds to your self-blaming by kindly reminding you of the real reason for your difficulties and you still don't feel convinced, try following this mini "CARE" strategy that got Gerry back on a positive track. It will help you to do some- thing constructive about your weaknesses and make a more rational assessment of the part they may have played in your current situation.

CARE STRATEGY FOR WEAKNESSES

Step 1: Care

Indulge yourself with some quality, sensual self-nurturing. This will distract your attention away from your weaknesses, reboot your self-esteem and reset your mind into a positive mode. Refer to Section 1 in this book if you're not sure how to do this!

Step 2: Action

Now make some serious resolutions. This will help you take constructive action to correct the weaknesses which can be changed or become more accepting of those you must learn to live with.

Draw two columns on a piece of paper. In the first, write out a list of your weaknesses and in the second note down the action you intend to take in relation to them. There will be some that you wish to work on because they are hindering your progress, but there will be others that you may wish to accept and find a more comfortable way of living with or avoiding situations where they might hold you back.

Here's Gerry's list:

WEAKNESS	ACTION
Age	Accept and focus on its benefits, e.g. wisdom
Being too soft with people	Assertiveness training
Shy – not good in big groups	Accept and do one-to-one and small-group networking; avoid big social events
Workaholic	Make firm rules about working hours and ask colleagues to help you abide by them

Step 3: Reappraise

Having engaged your rational mind and uplifted your mood you will be better placed to assess the true bearing your weaknesses have on your current situation. Draw a pie chart indicating the proportion of responsibility for your current problems that should be allocated to your weaknesses.

Step 4: Extol

Finally, you need to reboot your self-esteem and rebalance your view of yourself. A quick way to achieve this is to do a little private boasting about your virtues. Make a list of your personal strengths and read them aloud. Then finish by stating (again out loud) some of the positive action you have already taken to pull yourself through this tough patch in your life. Below are Gerry's lists of strengths and achievements as an example.

Gerry's strengths

✓ I face up to problems and snap into action fast.

✓ am kind and helpful.

✓ am prepared to learn and adapt to changing circumstances.

✓ have a great sense of humour and can amuse others.

✓ have survived many other setbacks and learnt from them.

Gerry's achievements since being made
redundant

✓ have allowed myself time to recover
emotionally and physically from the shock
and stress.

✓ have asked for help in spite of my
embarrassment about asking for it.

✓ have started to do an appraisal of my
finances (or career opportunities or social
situation etc.).

✓ am dealing more constructively with my
weaknesses.

ACTIVATE YOUR INNER TEAM

With different people and in different situations most of us can behave and feel quite differently. Indeed the differences can be so great that sometimes it feels as though we are a variety of different people rather than just one person. Take these people, for example:

"You should see me at work – I'm "Mr Fix-it" there. I'm a different person. I manage a team and a tight budget. At home, my wife sorts out and plans everything. She says I'm better playing with the children because I can't organise anything without forgetting something important or annoying someone."

"My friends say I'm a great listener and they all come to me with their problems. But with my boyfriend, I'm different. Sounds dreadful but I have no patience when he's down and my sister says I'm the same with her."

"Looking at the 360-degree feedback from my colleagues, you'd think I had no sense of humour. They seem to think I'm too serious. Yet my friends call me the joker in their pack."

"You should have seen me haggling in the market in Tangiers last year. I was the ace negotiator then. So why do I always end up giving in to the kids?"

There are many good reasons for being different people in different situations. For example, some aspects of personality are more appropriate to what you are trying to achieve, others are simply a better "fit" with what another person needs from you, and sometimes it is just more relaxing to switch into a different mode. Compartmentalising yourself in this way may be fine while things are going well. In difficult times, however, you cannot afford to sideline any of your strengths and skills and should aim for them all to be functioning in co-ordination with each other.

An interesting way of doing this is to think of your different "selves" as a team. As any good leader knows, the art of success is to create a group of people with different aptitudes and talents. This is because most problems need a variety of approaches and skills. But a good manager will ensure that the team has plenty of everyday practice working constructively together before sending them into a "fire-fighting" situation.

The exercise opposite is designed to help you to apply this team-training approach to the different parts of yourself. Repeat it a number of times with different examples; the principles will then stick fast in your brain so that your "team" is ready for action whenever it meets a challenge.

GETTING YOUR INNER TEAM INTO ACTION

Make a list of the different "people" you have within your personality. Next, choose an everyday real-life or hypothetical problem for them to sort out together. Assign a task to each "person" according to their special aptitudes or talents as in the example below.

Sample problem

My computer has crashed again. Is it worth upgrading to a new one, even though I'm strapped for cash right now? My IT knowledge is virtually nil – I dread the hassle of making this decision.

Plan

Your caring listener
Allow yourself to let off steam by kicking around some cushions and having a good "It's-not-fair" moan. Then plan a small comforting treat for now and an enticing reward for when you have made your decision!

Your helpful humourist

Get the problem into proportion by doodling a cartoon about yourself and your panic over it.

Your clever intellectual

Research the Internet for various options of new computers; gather feedback and assess its value.

Your friendly social networker

Search among your contacts for IT specialists who may have advice or other contacts; go to a computer shop and start up conversation with staff or customers who look at home; talk a "knowledgeable someone" into acting as your negotiator if you need one.

Your creative artist

Compose a colourful email that will have impact and instant appeal to friends and colleagues for help and advice.

Your sensible budgeter

Calculate comparative costs of different models and repair costs of current model and different interest on loans. Look at making cuts in other expenses.

Your efficient organiser/leader/manager

Do a timed action plan for your inner team. (They can't

all act at once!) Set a deadline for decision time. When all tasks are done if you still can't make the decision yourself, delegate the task to someone you trust who can and give your reward to them instead.

STRENGTHEN YOUR SELF-RELIANCE

When a crisis hits are you more likely to:
A) immediately turn to someone else, saying "Help . . . what should I do?"
or
B) go quiet and think to yourself, "Hell, how do I get through this?"

I know for sure that when I am faced with a big problem and thrown into my autopilot mode I am a B responder. This programmed character trait is another legacy of my childhood. I had to frequently fend for myself at a very early age, so developed a strong self-reliant streak which has undoubtedly helped me to bounce back from the many serious setbacks I have experienced. Interestingly, research findings show that the most likely people to survive disasters are those who do not expect to be rescued. They are the people who, in the heat of the crisis, automatically respond (as I am sure I would) with the thought: "What can I do to save myself in this situation?"

If you are more of an A responder, however, don't worry too much. You have one big advantage in that you find it easy and natural to ask for and use help. In the early days of a big crisis, such as immediately after bereavement, this is especially valuable. It gives you time to recoup your physical and emotional strength, while others get on with sorting out at least some of your preliminary practical problems.

Of course, unfortunately, help and support have a habit of gradually dwindling away if a problem situation drags on for any length of time. This is especially true in today's individualistic, competitive and busy world. Even the kindest of "helpers" have to (or feel they have to) keep their compassion in check. Almost every casualty of bereavement, chronic sickness, redundancy or divorce that I have ever met talks about this phenomenon. And it is at this point in a problematic situation that you most need to be able to draw on self-reliance. Those who will not readily accept this fact of modern life and cannot switch themselves into B mode are in danger of sliding into a powerless state. Feeling abandoned and rejected, they can become depressed, cynical and bitter. And, of course, these kinds of mental states do nothing at all to help them thrive or even survive through difficulties.

HOW TO SWITCH YOURSELF INTO SELF-RELIANCE MODE

Think twice before asking for help or advice

This sounds obvious, but you may be stuck in a habit and not realise how often you do this – and how unnecessarily. To remind yourself, put some sticky notes around your home, near your phones or computer or wherever else you think it would help you to fix this message in your mind.

Request advice in a confident way

Rather than asking questions that call for definite direction, such as: "What do you think I should do?" or "If you were in my shoes, would you...?", say something like: "I am trying to make a decision about what to do. It would really help to talk through the options I have thought of and also consider any other ideas you may have."

Politely deflect direct advice-givers

When you hear, "You should..." or "You must..." be ready to

gently raise your hand to indicate that you would like the advice-giver to stop. The earlier you can do this the better, but you may have to wait for a natural pause to emerge. Then say something like: "Thanks so much for your concern. That's *probably* good advice, but I really do need to think this through myself. I must be clear in my mind which is the right response/action/priority for me."

Please note the use of *"probably"*. You are not saying that their advice *is* good. You are only suggesting that it could be. Doing this preserves your right to disagree and not take their advice, but in such a way that the person doesn't feel rejected. If he or she persists in telling you what to do, then beware; they may have an over-controlling streak in their personality. Other phrases that you can use to achieve the same effect are: "That is a possible way forward"; "That could be a good idea"; "You might be right"; "Perhaps so"; "There could be some truth in that view".

Say an assertive, but polite, "No" to unnecessary offers of help

Should someone say, "I'll give them a ring for you," respond with: "Thanks so much for the offer, but I will ring myself." If the helper is pleased, rather than offended by your response, you will know that they are just the kind of person you need right now. Tell them you are trying to be more self-reliant and ask them to help you achieve this goal.

View mistakes as opportunities to become braver

"Take chances, make mistakes. That's how you grow. Pain nourishes your courage. You have to fail in order to practise being brave."

....

Mary Tyler Moore, actress and producer

Fear of "getting it wrong" is one the main things that holds people back from becoming more self-reliant – staying overly dependent on others is a way of avoiding responsibility for any possible negative outcome.

GIVE VOICE TO YOUR VALUES

. . . .

"If your morals make you dreary, depend upon it, they are wrong."

. . . .

Robert Louis Stevenson, nineteenth-century writer and poet

Self-respect is crucial for psychological health. It is not possible to have genuine self-esteem or self-belief without it. In addition to loving and taking excellent care of yourself, you need to be able to look in the mirror and see someone whom you can also truly respect.

But how is self-respect achieved?

Unfortunately, most of us learn about respect the hard way. A decisive moral awakening for me came from one of my daughters when she was just eleven. I shall never forget the stinging retort she gave me in response to a demand for

more respect: "Respect has to be earned, Mother!" Although
at the time this felt like a cheeky "below-the-belt" blow,
on later reflection I could see that it was well deserved.
Its wisdom still impacts upon my conscience today, and it
resounds in my head whenever I need reminding that, just
like the respect we have for anyone else, self-respect has to
be built on living proof. It isn't enough to believe in certain
moral standards; you must know that you are living by
them. This means that when you reflect on your behaviour,
your decision-making and your lifestyle, you must be able
to see the proof that your actions have been truly in sync
with principles you value. Good intentions do not bring
self-respect. Anyone who has felt the shame that comes
with repeating the same resolution with each new year
knows this well enough.

Difficult times frequently confront you with what you really
value in life. They are renowned for their ability to act
as a "wake-up call". Although no fallible human can ever
maintain moral perfection, true self-respect is only possible
if you are convinced that you are doing your very best to
live up to your principles.

The best tip for living in line with your own principles is to
compile a list of simple life rules. These can then be used
as an ever-ready checklist whenever you are confronted

by any kind of dilemma. As an example, I've shared three of my own below. These life rules have been immensely valuable for me. They work because they were especially created with my particular needs and bad habits in mind – see the comments in brackets. Your life rules would need to be similarly tailored especially for you.

My life rules are:

- to ask myself regularly if I am being true to my real self and my own values (I spent too many years trying to be someone I thought others wanted me to be)

- to spend more time than I think I can afford on relationships that matter most to me (I used to find it hard to say no to anyone who asked for my help, friendship or time; the result was that my close relationships suffered and I was getting burnt out)

- to see the positive in change, however unwelcome it may be (my programmed auto-response to change is depression, even though I have an excellent record of adjustment).

Try creating similar rules for yourself, but remember the following:

- They should feel **uplifting rather than burdensome**. To be motivating, they must bring you more pleasure than pain, so abiding by them should not feel in any way punishing!

This is important because so often there has been an early childhood association between morality and punishment which is etched deep into the neural system. (So remember the wise words of Robert Louis Stevenson quoted at the start of this tip.)

- They should be **relevant**. They need to fit with your current needs and priorities. This means they will need to be reviewed and possibly changed during or after each life transition or big experience. Most parents, for example, feel that they have to modify their guiding principles once their children come along. Other people say that they have to do this when they reach positions of leadership when it may be more appropriate to take a more conciliatory stance on many issues. During difficult times, you often have to be more compromising than you would otherwise be and this prompts a review of your principles.

- They should be **defendable**. They have to be able to stand up to the rigour of a "devil's advocate" test. You can do this for yourself, but you will have even more confidence in your principles if you can test them out with other people. To do the test on your own, use a two- chair exercise, whereby you start by sitting on one chair and making your case for your belief in one rule, then sit in the chair opposite you and take the stance of someone who believes the opposite. To do the test with someone else, ask a friend to take the role of devil's advocate or, if you are brave, you could start a debate with someone you know who you think truly does have opposite views from you.

- They should be **publishable.** In other words, they should not give you any cause for embarrassment. They need to reflect values that you are proud to be seen to uphold. If they do not, they will deplete rather than enhance your self-respect and self-belief.

Another way of putting your life rules through a rigorous test is to read books or articles on the Internet which express different views from yours.

Most people find that between three and six guiding life rules listed in hierarchical order is ideal – few enough to commit to memory, but enough to cover the key moral issues that will confront you. If you find it a struggle to come up with a list (and many people do at first attempt) this simple exercise will help you to clarify your key values.

YOUR PERSONAL HEROES

1. Make a list of about ten people you admire. These can be: people in your own personal life, such as family, friends or colleagues; famous people, dead or alive; fictional characters from books, films, TV or computer games.

2. Make notes on what it is or was about their behaviour, their lifestyle and their achievements that you admire.

3. Beside each name put down three to six value adjectives that you would associate with them as in the examples below:

    -   Nelson Mandela – courageous, persistent, flexible, visionary, humble

    -   Florence Nightingale – kind, persistent, pioneering, humble

    -   Superman – helpful, unusual, strong, ordinary at heart

    -   Grandmother – tolerant, modest, hard-working, resilient

When you have finished, see if you notice any similarities in these people and the way they lead/led their lives (imaginary or otherwise); usually, people find some even if there is not a repetition of the exact words. So, using the example above, the themes that emerge could be: being of service to others, resilient in the face of problems and confident and successful but not arrogant.

By this stage of the exercise, you should be starting to get ideas about the life rules you might want to make for yourself. If you still need some help, try doing the exercise with a friend. This should help you both to clarify your values especially if you play the devil's advocate game (p. 118).

1. Finally, you need to put your rules through some real-life tests. When you are faced with your next dilemma, use them as a reference guide. If they feel helpful and bring results that give you a sense of pride, they are right for you. If they fail this test, don't give up; it may take time to find a set that works for you.

"It has taken thirty-three years and a bang on the head to get my values right."

....
Sir Stirling Moss, world champion racing driver

QUICK FIX:
Stifle your selfish survival response with good deeds

Dousing the Protectionism Flames

Newspaper headline during the global financial crisis, 2009]

Twenty leaders from different countries gathered in London on the day of this news story. Their aim was to find ways of collaborating in order to solve the world's economic problems, as it was clear that "protectionism" (i.e. national selfishness) is one of the greatest obstacles to achieving this goal.

In difficult times, most people naturally prioritise looking after their own, but in the long term, there is a hefty price to be paid for this "survival-of-the-fittest" impulse. Your self-respect will plummet and your relationships with your community will deteriorate.

One way to guard against this happening is to make it

a rule for yourself to do one good deed each day, and record your act of kindness in a small notebook or in a file on your computer. You may not keep to your rule each day, but the monitoring process will prevent any selfish protectionist trend from getting its grip on you.

Your record can also serve as a more general self-esteem-boosting resource. Look at it whenever you need a reminder that you are actually "nice" occasionally!

GET A GRIP ON YOUR GUILT

"Every man is guilty of all the good he didn't do."

....

Voltaire, writer and philosopher

My own struggle to live with this tricky emotion started very young. I was brought up in convents which was tough on an adventurous child who found sinning very exciting. But I became cunning and was rarely found out. I largely avoided the cruel caning that so many of my friends endured, but my punishment lasted longer. It came in the form of persistent internal guilt. This feeling gnawed away at my self-esteem and was partly responsible for much of the self-destructive behaviour that nearly destroyed my life in early adulthood.

So not surprisingly, when I later become a psychotherapist, I developed a special interest in this topic. Almost every client I have ever had has been troubled in some way by guilt. I have seen it sabotage the efforts of many able people when they are in the midst of difficulties. They plague themselves with obsessive self-questioning and self-blame, tending to feel overly responsible for their problems.

DEALING WITH GUILT

Key 1: Stop wishing your guilt away

Accept that, unless you are a psychopath without a conscience, guilt is going to be one of life's companions! As is the case with any irritating "companion" you are stuck with, it is your responsibility to find a way of managing the relationship. No magic wand can make it disappear.

Key 2: Label guilt as "True" or "False"

True guilt is when you know you have done something which is not in line with your own moral code. This kind of feeling is a positive force. Its function is to produce enough discomfort to prompt you back on to the straight and narrow. It also curtails arrogance, and psychologists believe that it evolved in order to enable us to work co-operatively in groups as our tasks and problems were becoming more complex and too challenging for one individual.

False guilt is the kind you may feel even when your intellect and moral code tell you that you have done no wrong. This kind of feeling is usually triggered by someone else's real or imagined disapproval. A classic example for women today is when they feel guilty for leaving their children in the care of someone else to go out to work, while for men, it is when they feel guilty because they have had to accept sustenance from someone else because they have no means to feed, clothe or educate their family. In both cases, such "guilt trips" are often linked to values which were absorbed at an impressionable age from parents or grandparents or the more general influence of a culture or religion.

False guilt can also be an irrational symptom of people in a state of grief or depression. An example of this would be the "survivor guilt" felt by many Jews after the Holocaust or by families of people who have died in an accident or disaster. Another example of false guilt emerging in difficult times is when a recession causes a sharp rise in redundancies. Those who have managed to keep their jobs while so many around them have lost theirs are sometimes plagued by guilt.

Both true and false guilt can have debilitating and demotivating effects, and as they often feel the same, even very bright, self-aware people may confuse the two. Correct labelling of the emotion is essential because the action we need to take for each kind is different. You may need help to do this from someone you can trust to be objective and honest.

Key 3: Take appropriate action

Action for true guilt

Say sorry and spell out what you have learnt and intend to do differently as a result. Make recompense in the best way you can. For example, you may not be able to undo what you said or did, but you could send flowers, do a good turn or send a donation to an appropriate charity. Give yourself a self-esteem boost (see Mini-boosts, p.142).

Action for false guilt

Identify the cause of the false guilt and remind yourself of your own guiding moral code and life priorities (see p.125).

Next, compose a "permission" sentence that counters the unwanted moral message in your subconscious mind. It should remind you of one of your own good moral traits and a basic human right. For example, "I strive to be a good parent and have a right to make my own mind up about the wrong and right way to bring up my children." Or, "I am a compassionate and generous person even if I am exercising my right to work/be happy/live when others cannot." Write your sentence out again twenty times, then, with a calm, firm voice, read it aloud. This may sound boring and punitive, but it does work. Repetition is the key to programming moral directives into your mind. But in this exercise, you are in the director's chair. Each time you feel your false guilt resurface repeat your sentence several times in your head.

If your false guilt remains persistent it may mean that it relates to an unhealed emotional wound, in the way that the survivor guilt mentioned above does. The answer then is to see a therapist or counsellor or read my self-help book, *The Emotional Healing Strategy*.

ASK FOR COMPLIMENTS EVEN WHEN YOU KNOW YOU HAVE DONE WELL

A temporary swallowing of your humility is required while you read this tip, something that could be quite a challenge for British readers! Being bad at receiving compliments is just one of those habits that takes time and effort to break. It was deeply entrenched in my personality for the first thirty years of my life, but I'm I am proud to say that there is not a trace of it left. I feel only pure pleasure now when someone tells me that I have done well or that I am looking good.

So how did I achieve this transformation? It was sheer persistence with the advice I was given in assertiveness training. Firstly, I gave myself endless practice at just listening attentively to the compliments, allowing them to be absorbed and then replying with a simple, "Thank you". Then, when I found that this response didn't leave me friendless, I began to add an extra sentence of self-appreciation, such as, "Yes, I was pleased with the way I did that – I felt it was quite an achievement."

After a few weeks of practice, I found that I could take the super-assertive step of asking for a clarifying expansion of the compliment, for example: "What was it about the way I did it that you thought worked well?"

And finally, I reached the peak of compliment-gathering. I started to take the big risk and proactively "fish" for compliments even when I felt I didn't need them because I was certain I had done well. For example, after giving a talk that I can tell has gone down well with the audience, I might say to the organiser: "I feel pleased with the way that went, but I'd really like to know what you think." The vast majority of the time, the answer is one that will fluff up my feathers a little more, but I may get some negative feedback as well. This, of course, can be useful, and I probably would never hear it if I didn't asked for others' opinions.

This particular personal development journey has been one of the hardest I have ever had to take, but the rewards have made it worth it. Try taking the steps I've just described if you struggle to allow compliments to soak into your self-esteem. Compliments will help to immunise you against wounds to your pride and build self- confidence. And we all need many more of them during difficult times. You should never be embarrassed about taking or asking for them. And, of course, you should take care not to forget to give them out freely, even to people who appear not to need them.

QUICK FIX:
Welcome the wisdom you are gaining

A single conversation with a wise man is better than ten years of study.

Chinese proverb

Whenever you feel your confidence is rocky and you are not sure whether you can take (or even survive!) the next step, do the following:

- Recall the last failure, semi-failure or hurtful experience you had. Think of at least one thing you learnt as a result, for example: that your strengths are not organisational and you are better at nurturing people; that there isn't a market for . . . and that potential customers asked for more . . . ; that not everyone likes a hug when they cry.

- Think of one piece of wisdom you could gain from having to live through a potentially daunting experience. For example, perhaps your current problem is an enforced career change, living on your own or a drop in your standard of living. Although you may prefer not to have to face this kind of challenge, highlighting a potential gain in wisdom could help you to approach it a little more positively.

MIMIC YOUR MOANS AWAY

This may sound strange coming from someone who specialises in building self-esteem. But I do believe that laughing at yourself occasionally can be very useful.

This tip works in the same way as a little gentle teasing from a good friend or partner. I know that a bit of mimicking from my husband about my "long face" or "whiny" tone of voice can make me smile and snap myself out of the blues. You need to choose your moment sensitively though to humorously tease a loved one in this way – and the same is true for using this tip on yourself. It won't work if you are still very depressed, grieving or angry; when you are on the recovery road though and have just slipped off track a little, it can be very useful. So if you are aware (or have been made aware) that you are being a bit too gloomy for your own good, try this.

Stand in front of a full-length mirror and take a long, hard look at your body language. You may notice that your mouth is turning down slightly, that you are frowning or have let your shoulders droop. Next, exaggerate this body language and start to whine about your problems in an irritating, squeaky voice. Rev up your performance until you start smiling at the "silly" image you see before you.

A variation of this technique can also be done with a friend or group of friends. You can have fun mimicking each other as we sometimes do in dramatherapy work- shops to lighten an overly heavy atmosphere. Or, if you happen to live near a hall of silly mirrors, you can get the same kind of boost by taking a trip there with a friend.

FREE YOUR MIND FROM AUTO-THOUGHTS

"Change your thoughts and you change your world."

Norman Vincent Peale, positive thinking guru and writer

Carl, a professional photographer in his early fifties, was driving home from a new friend's house in the country one evening. In a momentary lapse of concentration, he took a right turn instead of a left one and found himself facing oncoming traffic on a dual carriageway. The result was a crash in which a woman was killed.

Carl was given a fifteen-month prison sentence. He had not drunk any alcohol and had a clean twenty-three-year driving record. He had never been in any kind of trouble with the law before. A caring, sensitive and highly responsible man, he had never in his wildest nightmares thought that he would spend time in prison. He was terrified.

In order to help him cope with the devastating thoughts and feelings about what he had accidentally done and its consequences, Carl is constantly looking for ways to extract something positive out of his prison experience. This extract from one of his letters to me is an example:

"Deprived of society's usual distractions, I have nowhere to hide in the short term, in terms of facing my fears and some of my habitual thought patterns that I took for granted as being part of myself and my life. I have stepped out of the pattern of being continually lost in thought and any emotion that would trigger. I have learnt to stand back and witness my own thoughts as they are happening. This has given me a choice. I can choose to pay attention to the thought or let it pass. Before, I would give all thoughts equal weight and believe I would have to get to the bottom of all of them and their corresponding emotion – in effect, always to "solve" problems. It is hard to describe, but I have become able to witness my thoughts as a presence behind them, rather than being swept along by them without any awareness or wider choice. This is my freedom."

I believe Carl's strategy is one that can be used in many other difficult situations as well. When you go through hard times, it is easy to be at the mercy of thoughts that enter your mind without your conscious consent; they can make you feel fearful, guilty, pessimistic, regretful or even powerless, when the reality is that you are confident and capable enough to deal positively with your problem.

If this happens to you, remember Carl's trick of imagining himself as an observer of his thoughts, with the freedom to be able to choose which ones you will pursue and which you will let go.

You might also like to try a variation, which is to give your thoughts a pictorial representation. One of the most popular choices is to imagine the thoughts encircled by clouds. You can then decide to see them as heavy, grey ones or light, wispy ones set against a blue sky or the warm glow of a beautiful sunrise. Then it is up to you whether you choose to dwell on your thoughts or just let them drift slowly – or quickly – by.

REGAINING
CONTROL

In times of stress or crisis, it can be seem impossible to see the light at the end of the tunnel. The problems that we are experiencing can seem all-encompassing, but taking a step back to calm our minds and gain perspective is often not as hard as it initially seems. People often think that those who can stay cool and calm during difficult times are genetically privileged, while others will always be at the mercy of their moods and therefore have a harder time. The tips in this section should help to dispel this myth.

Emotional intelligence – a person's ability to understand their own (and others') emotions and to use them appropriately – is something that can be learnt by absolutely anyone, although it may take some a little longer to develop it than others; just how long will depend partly on your inherited temperament, as well as the amount of time you invest in finding out what does or does not work for you as an individual. This is partly why this section is the longest in the book – I wanted to include tips to suit all kinds of emotional predispositions, and the only way to know whether or not they will work for you is to try a range of them out.

The other reason why this section is the longest is because difficult times tend to generate a greater degree of feeling than normal, making them testing times even for those who usually manage their moods well. So you may well find that while your favourite ways of calming your- self down are not quite good enough in tough times, there are some new ideas here for you to try that will help you.

FEED A
PSYCHOLOGICAL
NEED

....

This is a great tip if you are in a panic about something. Perhaps your working life is threatened or your income could be drastically reduced for some other reason? Very often there is a period of time when you are powerless to do anything about a worrying situation other than wait, whether for news of a job or another change of financial wind.

But what you can do instead is to focus on feeding your psychological needs. This will divert your attention from your concerns about your material wealth, while strengthening your psychological health.

Here are some examples of psychological needs and how they can be "fed", simply by using the tips in this book. But remember, there are many other psychological needs and many other low-cost and quick ways to fulfil them.

PSYCHOLOGICAL NEED	FULFILLING TIP
Achievement	Power yourself into action with goals (p. 203)
Companionship	Deepen your key relationships (p. 52)
Adventure	Transform possibilities into inspirational goals (p. 22)
Status	Ask for compliments even when you know you have done well (p. 129)
Self-esteem	Drip-feed your self-esteem with mini-boosts (p. 142)
Reassurance	Use imaginary mentors to psych you up (p. 184)
Solitude	Create a ten-minute hibernation haven (p. 28)
Self-expression	Write a song (p. 181)
Self-determination	Strengthen your self-reliance (p. 110)

DRIP-FEED YOUR SELF-ESTEEM WITH MINI-BOOSTS

Most people don't realise that self-esteem is knocked back more by everyday events than by the big setbacks in life. For example, we can get used to being herded like cattle into trains, being ignored by shop attendants chatting to their friends or being left hanging on the end of the phone for 15 minutes. This kind of disrespect is so common and so impersonal that – sadly – it is rarely worth the hassle to "fight back". But it takes its toll, nevertheless. You can negate the emotional damage it causes, however, by counteracting it with equally regular mini-boosts which will instantly lift your self-esteem. Here are some examples:

SHARE GOOD NEWS HOWEVER SMALL

Ring a good friend and tell them about a mini-achievement, such as clearing your pending file, a spring clean, revamping your CV or resisting a temptation.

GIVE YOURSELF A TREAT EACH DAY

This could be a favourite food or drink, a walk in a garden, a ten-minute break to read or listen to music. Remember to vary the experiences though, otherwise they will begin to feel too routine.

LOG YOUR ACHIEVEMENTS

Writing down on paper or on the computer what you have achieved each day or week will fix these achievements more firmly in your brain; include both personal and work-related ones.

SPRUCE UP YOUR APPEARANCE EVEN WHEN YOU ARE SOLO

Make those glances in the mirror or reflections in shop windows as uplifting as they can be.

KEEP PHOTOS OF PEOPLE WHO LOVE YOU VISIBLE

Swap the positions of these from time to time so you notice them more.

GIVE COMPLIMENTS MORE FREELY

Find reasons to compliment others, but make sure they are genuine and not too general. The smile of the receiver will boost you too.

MAKE A SAVING

Say "No" to buying something you don't really need or wasting time, money and energy on doing something you don't need to do.

SHARE YOUR EMPATHY NON-VERBALLY

Just giving a sympathetic smile or raised eyebrows and a shake of the head to someone who looks sad or who has been treated disrespectfully can lift both your spirits and theirs. A few words may help too, but often they are not necessary and may not be appropriate.

CONSTANTLY CHECK WHETHER YOU OR YOUR AUTOPILOT IS IN CONTROL

Long before the birth of "emotional intelligence" wise people knew that control over your feelings was crucial for functioning well and being happy. Especially during hard times, you need to be fully aware of the kind of circumstances which might flip you out of control and into autopilot mode. When this happens, your head is out of a job. It is your feelings that are in the driving seat and you have no choice but to dance to a tune composed partly by your primitive "animal" self and partly by a set of neural connections which were haphazardly created through a combination of nature and nurture.

Although it is commonly said that the "true self" comes out when you lose your cool or are challenged by fear, in my opinion this is nonsense. Our emotional autopilots were, after all, hard-wired without our conscious consent. I know mine certainly was. When, for example, my emotional autopilot is in control, it makes an appalling mess of my life. This is because my original mental programming triggered a muddle of contradictory responses. This is not surprising – my parents' bitter and tragic personal war combined with the external pressures of the Second World War and the constant traumas of life in a succession of care homes programmed my auto- pilot to always act as though a major catastrophe is about to hit. This is why I remain alert to the possibility that, in certain circumstances, I will overreact and start to produce a package of confusing yo-yo behaviours that were "designed" *for* me, not *by* me. The job description of my autopilot is to deal with the threatened survival of a powerless child, not a confident and capable grown-up psychotherapist!

I am aware that my autopilot programming was not "normal". But I also know that there are many people whose autopilot is even less well equipped to deal with their real adult world. And, even if your nature and nurture were "blessed", they can't have been perfect. So we all need to take care when we enter into the danger zones which trip us into auto-emotional mode. Your feelings, whether they are good or bad, are not necessarily "the real you".

Difficult times tend to bring many of the circumstances that constitute an emotional danger zone into play. Your autopilot is likely to jump into the driving seat when you:

- are tired or physically weak due to illness or in pain

- are facing something that makes you frightened or very anxious

- think that you have been treated unfairly and are angry

- feel helpless and think you have no power to change the situation

- encounter someone or a situation that has echoes of a significant person or event in your past

- are in a highly excitable state – perhaps due to being "in love" or because you have an idea or project that you care "passionately" about.

Can you relate to any of the above right now? If not, you are lucky and should be prepared for your good fortune on this account to change. It can happen to literally anyone if they are put under enough pressure.

When you know you are in "at-risk" circumstances, ask yourself the following three questions:

1. Is what I am doing or saying appropriate for the here- and-now situation?

2. Is this feeling similar to one that I felt very deeply in the past?

3. Is this idea really a good intuition or simply a fear or irritation or attraction that has resurfaced from the past because my brain has encountered a reminder?

If you answer "No" to question 1, stop what you are doing as soon as possible. After taking some time out to de-stress your body, take time for a rethink.

If you answer "Yes" to questions 2 or 3, don't skip the next tip!

If you answer "Yes" to the first question, and "No" to the other two – again, continue reading. Firstly, it will help you to help others who may need support from your emotional strength. Secondly, you will at least be well prepared should your own circumstances become rocky one day.

"The most courageous decision you make each day is the decision to be in a good mood."

....

Voltaire, French writer and philosopher

QUICK FIX:
Rebalance your pulse with slow repetitive rhythm

Repetitive rhythms such as drumming, bell ringing or Gregorian chants have been used for centuries as calming devices. Today, contemporary relaxation specialists will use a wide variety of rhythmic sounds, such as recordings of natural rhythmic phenomena like lapping waves or specially composed electronic pieces, using steady beats that are heard by the subconscious mind.

You can create a good-enough effect instantly though, without any fancy musical equipment. When you feel your heart beating faster, just slow your pulse by closing your eyes and tapping your fingers or a pencil in a slow rhythmic way on something hard. If your attention wanders away back to your worries, take a couple of deep, slow breaths from the depths of your stomach and focus back on the sound of your tapping. Trust that your pulse will slow and it will.

GET A HANDLE ON YOUR "HARD DRIVE"

. . . .

"It's terrible – I can hear my mother's voice coming out of my own mouth! You know how I always swore I'd never be like her, but nowadays I'm irritable all the time. Last week, I even heard myself say, "If this carries on, I'll be back in hospital and then you'll be sorry!" Remember, my mother was only four years older than I am now when she died – you can't fight your genes."

. . . .

Carol, a breast cancer sufferer and mother of boys aged five and eight

Being a good parent was at the top of Carol's list of life goals when she first came to see me a few years ago. She went to a number of drama therapy weekends that I run and worked very successfully on developing her self-confidence. She used to be very quiet and unassuming, but for years had been managing well without any help: she had reached a senior management position at work, had a happy marriage, a new circle of close friends and had also become an excellent parent. Indeed, all was going as well as any of us can expect from life until three years ago. This was when Carol was diagnosed with breast cancer. Her initial treatment went well and her prognosis appeared to be good, but then another lump appeared. This time she was advised to have a mastectomy.

Bad as this health problem was, it did not seem to me to be enough to throw the "new" Carol so off course. So, I questioned her further. She then revealed that she had very strong suspicions that her husband was having an affair. He denied it, but she knew that their relationship had "not been the same" since the most recent breast crisis, and she now feared that this mastectomy would finally finish it. Worse still, she had a scenario running through her head that she could die soon and the boys would lose both parents if her husband had left.

With the shock and multiple stresses of her current life, Carol's "hard drive" (or autopilot) had taken control of her thinking and many of her responses. Because I knew about Carol's background, I could very quickly spot what was going on. I knew that reassuring comfort and problem-solving strategies would, at that moment, fall on deaf ears. Before she could use the resources of her intelligent mind and her supportive friends, she needed to get back in the driving seat of her own brain.

For those of us who are used to helping people through crises, there is nothing unusual about this situation. It can happen to any of us and, like Carol, we might not be aware of what is happening. It often takes confrontation from someone else who is both knowledgeable and assertive to make us realise that we are not in full control of our conscious thinking mind and our feelings. For Carol, it was a good friend who persuaded her to go back to me. As it happens, this was good for Carol because she had gone beyond the stage where she could pull herself out of her depressed rut. But the good news is that it didn't take long to do this together, mainly because

Carol already had so much self-awareness. She has now had her mastectomy and is considering reconstructive surgery. Her husband has agreed to couple counselling and I understand it is going well. Her friends organised a "babysitting rota" among themselves so that she has a break from the children twice a week. Her strength is returning day by day and she has negotiated with her employer that she can start back on flexi-time for the first six months. "New" Carol is well and truly back in charge!

To ensure that she keeps a handle on the negative ideas and responses on her hard drive, Carol did the opposite exercise with me. I have used extracts from hers as examples. Try it for yourself. (If you, like Carol, had what might be termed as "a very difficult childhood", you may need a few sessions with a therapist as well to help you achieve enough insight.)

Make a list of the key examples you came up with and keep it to hand as a warning. Look at it from time to time while you are going through a difficult period. And remember that they will surface when you are stressed. So first, you need to relax and recover, then pick up this book again to help you find something that will quickly reboot your morale and get you back into positive problem-solving mode.

Carol's hard drive reminder exercise

NEGATIVE RESPONSE	EXAMPLES	DERIVATION
Philosophising	Blood is thicker than water	Mum's fantasy
Self-talk	'You idiot'; 'You never learn'	Teacher's lack of faith
Feelings	Fear of change	No practice or role models as a child
Reactions to people	Submissive to authority	Repressive schooling; caning
Mind-reading	He must think I am...	Outsider as child/low self-esteem
Gloomy predictions	Knowing my luck...	Series of bad-luck experiences; early failures
Behaviour	Withdrawal; not speaking up; not asking for help	Dad; punishment

GET PREPARED FOR PANIC PARALYSIS

. . . .

"Anxiety is a bully – it takes from your life, and every concession you make to it, it takes more. It will never be enough."

. . . .

Catherine O'Neill, Awareness Manager at Anxiety UK

If you are prone to anxiety, difficult periods might provoke a panic attack. If you have never had one before and don't recognise the symptoms and how to deal with them, they can be very frightening. So frightening that you become anxious about having another attack, and so then, of course, you do!

Symptoms, which tend to occur very suddenly, without any warning and often for no apparent reason, include:

- the sensation that your heart is beating irregularly (palpitations)

- the sensation of being detached from the world around you (depersonalisation)

- sweating

- trembling

- hot flushes

- chills

- shortness of breath

- choking sensation

- chest pain

- nausea

- dizziness

- feeling faint

- numbness or pins and needles

- dry mouth

- a need to go to the toilet

- ringing in your ears.

Because the symptoms are often very intense, you may feel like you are having a heart attack or, worse still, dying. The fear of having a heart attack can then add to your sense of panic. If you need more convincing that every single one of these symptoms is consistent with an anxiety attack, consult your doctor or a reputable health information website.

The following strategy is based on the advice of Anxiety UK, a charity that helps those with anxiety disorders.

STRATEGY FOR DEALING WITH A PANIC ATTACK

Step 1: Reassure yourself with the facts

Use informed self-talk to quell the thoughts that have been produced by your feelings of fear. Here are some statements that will counteract the most common fears:

- **This is not dangerous. If this was a heart attack your symptoms would not reduce if you slowed your breathing, sat down or left the situation, as they often do when you are having a panic attack. All your other symptoms are normal physiological reactions during an attack of anxiety.**

- I am not going to collapse. Your blood pressure increases when you experience anxiety, making you less likely to faint.

- I can cope. You have a strategy and you are in control.

- I don't need to run away. You will gain control and if you run away the panic attack wins and will go on winning. People can and do carry on with highly responsible jobs while experiencing and controlling these symptoms. Nobody except you is likely to notice that you are having an anxiety attack.

- Panic attacks pass. No one can sustain a panic attack forever – usually they do not last for longer than an hour.

Step 2: Slow down your breathing

Take control of your breathing by doing the following exercise. Repeat until you feel your breathing has returned to normal.

1. Breathe in deeply from your diaphragm (count to 6) 2. Rest (count to 2)

2. Breathe out slowly (count to 12)

3. Rest (count to 2)

Step 3: Engage yourself in a distracting activity

To stabilise your breathing and take your mind off your attack, do something that distracts your attention away from your body. This could, for example, be work, a crossword, simply counting backwards from fifty or how many objects of a certain colour there are around you.

Step 4: Review your lifestyle

Check that you are giving yourself enough time to de-stress your mind and your body on a regular basis throughout the day. Almost all the tips in the first five sections of this book can help you to do this. But don't overwhelm your- self with different goals (a common mistake of anxious people); choose a few ideas that you think could particularly help you at the moment and make an action plan to help you to integrate them into your life.

Practise this strategy regularly and use it whenever you become aware of minor anxiety symptoms such as fluttering feelings in your stomach. If you do then have a panic attack, you will know the routine and apply it almost automatically.

PREVENT MOLEHILLS OF IRRITATION FROM GROWING INTO VOLCANOES OF RAGE

For twenty-five years, Steve had had his own plumber's merchant shop in the centre of town. He had inherited the business from his father and was well known and trusted in the community. When a large national DIY chain with a plumbing section opened in a commercial park on the outskirts of town, he was confident that it would not pose a threat. For several years, his business stayed stable, but when an economic downturn began to bite into the budgets of his clients, they were forced to put aside their loyalty and go for the superstore's lower prices.

Steve had always been renowned for being cheerful and unflappable. His staff found him a generous and easy-going employer. But as his financial worries increased, he became irritated by both his staff and his family. Things like his staff popping out for 10 minutes to get their cappuccinos, lights left on, his children's skateboards lying in the hall, their music playing too loudly and his wife's chatter on the phone to her sister all began to grate on his nerves. But he'd swallow down his irritation and say nothing. Eventually though, he would snap and lose his temper over "something and nothing". Steve was aware of what was at the root of his outbursts, so he would apologise profusely and make even more of an effort to stay calm in the face of these petty annoyances. But he did not seem to be able to change this pattern of behaviour and his outbursts continued.

His wife persuaded him to go to his GP to ask for something to calm his nerves. The doctor instead lent him my book *Managing Anger* from the surgery's library. As Steve is not a great reader, he contacted me instead. It seemed that as he had never suffered a short-fuse problem before, he just did not know how to handle the feelings that this new stressful situation had generated. The solution for him was some simple anger-management strategies. His difficult trading situation hasn't yet changed, but he has at least regained his usual emotional equilibrium and, as I write, is considering his options with the help of a small-business adviser.

It is very easy to let minor irritations build up when you have major problems to contend with. Even if you, like Steve, are normally good at responding assertively to people when they are annoying you, when you are stressed you often can't be bothered to "fight" these minor battles. To avoid a build-up of irritation, try following the three simple steps below. You must put them into action as soon as you notice that you are beginning to feel impatient or annoyed. The longer you leave even mild anger to fester, the harder it is to deal with later.

1. DEFUSE

Use simple physical actions such as deep breathing or clenching or unclenching your fists to send a message to your brain to switch off the anger response which has, among other auto-responses, caused your heart to start beating faster and your muscles to begin tensing up. Doing this will avoid a build-up of repressed feeling.

2. REVIEW

Now that you are physically calm, you can engage your
rational brain more easily to decide whether this is an issue
that you need to deal with or not.

3. CONFRONT
OR DIVERT

Confront by assertively saying something like: "I found
myself getting irritated when you..." (Note – you are just
communicating your feeling, not making an accusation).
Then make a request: "In future, would you please..."

Or, if you have chosen the divert option, find something
engrossing to do which will help you forget the incident.

QUICK FIX: |
Ask yourself to dance

Dancing is a wonderful way to let go of pent-up feelings and tension. And we also now know that it has benefits for the brain as well. A twenty-one-year study of senior citizens, aged seventy-five and older, at the Albert Einstein College of Medicine in New York City, found that dancing reduced the risk of dementia by an impressive 76 per cent.

At this point in time, you may not feel like going to clubs or other places where people are dancing just for fun. And in any case, a shortage of time and money may rule that option out. So why not invite yourself to dance in the privacy of your own home? You will reap exactly the same therapeutic benefits and maybe even more. One of the great advantages of secret solo dancing is that you can dance as wildly (and as badly!) as you like.

Better still, if you can create a safe enough space, try dancing with a blindfold on. It is an even more freeing and uplifting experience.

TAKE YOUR BRAIN
TO THE GYM

· ·

*"Live as if you were to die
tomorrow. Learn as if you were
to live for ever."*

· · · · · · · · · · · · · ·

Mahatma Gandhi, leader of the Indian
nationalist movement

Brain Gym (braingym.org.uk) is a programme of physical
exercises designed to stimulate brain activity that was
originally developed by Dr Paul Dennison and his wife
Gail in the 1970s and 1980s in the field of education in
California. Despite many controversies about the scientific
evidence for improving learning potential, Brain Gym is
still widely used in educational establishments around the
world and has many dedicated devotees.

I certainly do not claim to be an expert in this field, but
there are a few exercises which I have personally used to
good effect and have often suggested to clients. Below are a

couple of appropriate ones for difficult times. If these work for you, you might want to find out more about the theories and practice of Brain Gym. Don't be put off by the scarcity of hard scientific evidence and cynics; good practitioners in their field are often ahead of the academic game, and there certainly doesn't seem to be anything to lose by doing some experimentation and research.

CROSS-CRAWL

I like this exercise, not just because it is a great quick aerobic energiser, but also because it involves cross- lateral movements which help to stimulate the neural connections between the left and right brain hemispheres. So it is a great one for us writers when we get stuck with that infamous "writer's block". Many educationalists also use it on a regular basis to improve spelling, writing, listening, reading and comprehension.

1. Standing or sitting, put your right hand across your body to your left knee as you raise it, then do the same thing for the left hand on the right knee, just as if you were marching.

2. Continue for at least 2 minutes.

FLEX YOUR CHANGE MUSCLES

....

"A person needs at intervals to separate from family and companions and go to new places. One must go without familiars in order to be open to influences, to change."

....

Katherine Butler Hathaway, poet and children's writer (she spent ten years of her life on her back, due to polio)

Moving on from difficult times frequently demands that you make some kind of major change in your life. Major life changes could very well be:

- **a change in your living arrangements through restricted finances**

- **a family break-up or loss**

- a new medical condition or disability that needs to be accommodated

- needing to find a different kind of job

- new friends or a different partner

- a new psychological outlook or behaviour style.

Very few changes are easy rides, especially if they have been forced upon you, and it is human nature (even animal nature) to feel uncomfortable, frightened and often angry.

Where you have no choice in the matter and fighting back isn't an option, a common defence is to go into denial and say something like: "Well, it might not happen anyway, and if it does I'll cross that bridge when I come to it." But this kind of "head-in-the-sand", fatalistic approach makes adjusting to change even more difficult.

To make the best of change, you have to embrace it confidently and positively. As someone whose whole life has been constantly peppered by change, I know that this does get easier (but still not easy) the more it happens. You become more accepting of emotional turmoil and are more wised-up on how to manage the feelings. You also learn to empower yourself by taking as much control as you can over the way the change happens. And, very importantly, you look after yourself better by taking lots of support while you are making the adjustment.

You'll cope better still with the bigger and more frightening changes if you keep your "change muscles" well exercised. A little practice at making some small adjustments in your life, your way of doing things or your outlook can help you to feel much more at ease when it comes to weathering the bigger transitions.

Below are some examples of the practical "homework" exercises that I suggest to clients who know they have to take a big leap forward into some kind of new life or lifestyle. Keeping some notes on how you felt before, during and after the change is very useful. Not only do you find out what helps and what doesn't, you also become more aware of what to expect in terms of your emotional reaction.

SUGGESTIONS FOR GENTLY FLEXING YOUR CHANGE MUSCLES

- Read a bestselling book that you wouldn't normally be attracted to.

- Visit somewhere you have never been to and, if possible, use a different method of transport to make the journey.

- Eat out at a restaurant or café that serves a kind of food you have never tried before.

- Go to a religious service or ritual occasion of a faith you know very little about.

- Participate in a festival from another culture.

- Try a sport that you have never tried; those that involve others work best. Most clubs or associations will be only too willing to let you try your hand.

- Do an activity with people from a different age group.

- Make an extravagant purchase if you are normally frugal.

- Live on next to nothing for a week if you have a relatively comfortable income.

- Go to the cinema on your own (unless you already do so).

- Change your hairstyle or colour.

- Exchange some household tasks with other members of the family.

Finally, as you go through your changes, notice how you as a person are subtly adjusting and developing. For me, that is the most exciting part of moving on and I am still constantly surprised by the way change can change me and others. If you manage your transitions well, the change in you is sure to be a positive one that will enrich your life.

"The most important thing to remember is this: to be ready at any moment to give up what you are for what you might become."

....

W. E. B. du Bois, civil rights activist

BORE YOUR BRAIN INTO DAYDREAM MODE

. . . .

Every time you let yourself slip into a daydream, your brain starts to work in an important way on your behalf. Neuroscience has revealed that it goes into a mode that is now thought to be its "default network", and while in this state, certain interconnected areas are activated. This particular kind of activity makes new connections between seemingly unrelated ideas and information. As a result, new perceptions and ideas generate creative activity.

I have known about the creativity-boosting potential of daydreaming for many years. However, I have always thought that this very useful mental state is best induced through deep relaxation, which usually entails setting aside a sizeable chunk of time in order to unwind – and even more time if you happen to be stressed out by the kind of problems that tough times can bring.

So I was very interested to learn that the research now indicates that this default network is most often activated when we are engaged in performing routine tasks that require very little conscious attention or when we are listening to something that we find rather boring. If your everyday life is anything like mine then you will no doubt be able to think of many examples of such tasks:

- Clearing up after a meal

- Standing in a queue at the supermarket, station or airport

- Travelling on public transport when it is too noisy and busy to be able to use the time for reading or listening to music

- Going to a boring lecture or presentation which is delivered with a deadly drone

- Attending a routine meeting, just to show your face

- Watching a film at the cinema that you find boring but which your companion is glued to

- Sweeping away leaves or snow in the garden

- Waiting in a doctor's surgery

- Ironing

So you can now let your mind have a guilt-free wander when you find yourself in one of these situations. Indeed, Arthur Fry, inventor of the sticky yellow Post-it notes, is said to have come up with his very clever idea while daydreaming through a tedious sermon.

There is just one catch though: you must retain some conscious control over your daydreaming. In order for this state to be productive, you need to be aware enough of what you are doing to be able to notice a bright idea. This is why daydreaming while still engaged in some kind of task – even if that is only listening with half an ear – is better than floating off into a less conscious state.

If you happen to be the kind of person who is never bored and who is lucky enough to have someone else to do all your mindless chores for you, read the previous tip on napping!

QUICK FIX:
Be wary of nostalgia

Research has revealed that the brain is very selective about the memories it stores. For example, it favours the best and worst of times, and also has something of an obsession with endings. So if an outcome was eventually good (such as first holding your newborn), that is the memory that will be clear and bright. Your memory of the long, drawn-out labour, the sweat and tears will be recorded minimally in comparison.

Of course, indulging in nostalgia can sometimes make you feel good, but in difficult times, it can leave you with feelings of regret that today can't be as good.

Remember also that consistent, lasting happiness is not always punctuated with ecstatic, memorable moments, which means that we are less likely to recall it.

So whenever you find yourself regretting that you can't turn the clock back, remind yourself that your brain might have got it wrong, and return your focus to doing all you can to make your present and future as rewarding as they can be.

MAKE A
DRAMA OUT
OF YOUR
DREAM

· · · · · · · · · · · · · · · ·

Thirty-five-year-old Teresa was someone who had apparently drifted haphazardly into a number of different careers. Three months before I saw her she had been told that it was possible that there would be a departmental restructure in the near future. Having heard this euphemism before, she knew that this was a strong hint that her job was at risk. Her boss kindly suggested that when Teresa considered her next job move, she should ensure she takes some time out first to help her make a well- thought-through career decision rather than a desperate jump into the first option that came available.

Teresa was persuaded by a friend to join her on one of my "Moving On" courses in Spain. She started by saying that she didn't want to waste our time as she didn't think there was much hope of her changing: "I'm a starter and not a finisher," she said. "I get all these ideas and have all these dreams about what I could do, but I never follow through on my plans."

We used psychodrama to explore the root cause of her motivational problem which lay mostly in her busy, harassed parents' lack of interest in her development and success. Then the group helped her to bring her dream career to life.

Since travelling around the world in her early twenties, Teresa had dreamed about having her own specialist travel agency. So we played out various highly positive scenarios with Teresa in the star role as owner of an eco- tourism agency, offering holidays in Africa. Then, later that evening, the group threw her a celebration party. They pretended she had won a Business Woman of the Year award. They toasted her with sparkling wine and made a giant celebration poster. One person took the role of playing the High Commissioner of Uganda and presented her with a colourful certificate that had been painted by another participant.

On her return home, Teresa pinned her certificate up in her bedroom, together with photos of the celebratory event the group had organised. This helped her recall and relive the wonderful fun she'd had with them enacting her dream. Several group members kept in contact with her, enquiring as to how her career dream plans were developing.

Teresa is now working for a travel company operating safaris in Africa with a view to learning the trade. She is having a wonderful time and appears to have an aptitude for the business. She believes that the dramatisation of her dream totally changed both her and her life.

Psychodrama is just one way that can help you to make a drama out of your dream. But it is certainly not the only way. You could invite your friends over for a "dream drama party", which would work just as well as a motivator.

CREATIVE VISUALISATION

You can also use creative visualisation to bring your dream to life by creating a motivating drama in your head. Here are six simple steps to help you do this:

1. Find as quiet a place as possible. Ideally, this would be in a private, sound-proofed room where you could lie down and close your eyes. But if this is not available, just stay standing or sitting where you are in a relaxed posture. This would mean uncrossing any crossed limbs, putting both feet on the ground and ensuring that your body feels balanced and supported in the best way it can be.

2. Take deep slow breaths while focusing your mind on your breath going in and out of your body. The out-breath should be a little longer than the in-breath, and it is helpful to stay in "pause position" for a few seconds between the in- and out-breaths. This should take you into a deeply relaxed state, but one in which you are still aware and conscious.

3. Use your imagination to visualise your dream coming true. Notice all the details in your visualisation such as:

- the colours, sounds and shapes

- the people and objects around

- yourself – how do you look? How do you sound? And, very importantly, try and sense how you are feeling and reacting in this scene.

1. Imagine that you can turn up the definition of the visualisation. Increase the volume and brightness and the sensations and relax even more, giving yourself up to the experience without thinking or judging it. Just enjoy it.

2. Bring yourself back into the world by taking a couple of deep breaths and having a stretch.

3. Repeat this visualisation two or three times over the coming week to ensure that the "false memory" of your dream being realised is firmly planted in your subconscious mind.

WRITE A SONG

Another idea might be to write a song about the realisation of your dream and sing it regularly to yourself. This worked particularly well for one of my clients, especially as her dream was to become a professional songwriter! She has now reduced her job to a three-day week and writes and performs on the other two days.

These kinds of creative techniques will increase your motivation because they "trick" your mind into thinking that achieving your dream is much more of a real possibility because it has "happened" before. Sports stars have been using them for years. Even if you are not looking for a radical change of career or lifestyle at the moment, this tip could still give you some other benefits: they are fun and confidence-building too.

MOVING
ON

In the immediate aftermath of a crisis, you often get a surge of energy, and the extra shot of adrenalin that your body creates helps to keep you going. However, the later "moving-on" process can sometimes seem to drag on interminably, and it can be especially hard to keep going forward positively if you have little control over the outcome or when you have no idea as to how long a problem will take to resolve.

Even when you do have control over the goals and action plans that you set for yourself, the process of achieving them is rarely straightforward; you may already have found yourself feeling that your progress is one step forward and two steps back.

At the same time, you may find that you are starting to feel less supported by others. The initial rally of back-up from friends and family may well have receded by now, just at the time when your adrenalin charge has subsided, leaving you feeling overwhelmed and badly in need of reassurance and comfort.

If you are now at that point where you have to pick up the pieces of your old life or forge a new and challenging path-way, it's likely that you'll be feeling much more alone than you did earlier on in your crisis. It is now that you need to be able to draw on a "tool-box" of self-help strategies to help you remain on or return to a positive course. The tips in this section will give you those tools; they will boost your spirits, calm your fears and eradicate some of the bad habits and stress that may be affecting your momentum. Finally, there is also an exercise that will help you to formulate a simple action plan and select your own three top tips from this book to kick-start you into action.

USE IMAGINARY MENTORS TO PSYCH YOU UP

· · · · · · · · · · · · · · · ·

"Don't be too sad. I went through some rough ones as well. One was here on this court last year ... and I came back and won. You're an unbelievable guy ... you are going to come back and win it. I really hope so."

· · · · · · · · · · · · · ·

Roger Federer, tennis champion
(to his opponent, Andy Roddick)

Not all major winners in life are as generous and supportive as Roger Federer, but I do believe that although they may not get a chance to demonstrate this so publicly, very many others are. And although you may not be lucky enough to have such people at your side in real life right now, you can use your imagination to trick your emotional system into reacting as though you do; because your brain doesn't know the difference between real and imagined events, it will produce the same good feeling that hearing encouragement in real life from some of life's winners would bring.

Here's what to do:

- Compile a list of three to six people whom you admire for their persistence through times of difficulty. They could be people you know or famous figures (see the list of quotes below for inspiration). If possible, include one or two who have faced the same kind of challenge that you are facing. When I was facing a major financial challenge, for example, I used my great-grandfather; he made and lost and regained many millions several times. I am sure if he had been there he would have given me perspective and some hope that my genetic inheritance might kick in! Similarly, when my daughter died, I recalled the faces of Isabel Allende, whose daughter also died, and Nelson Mandela, whose son died while he was on Robben Island. I have never been lucky enough to meet any of these courageous and generous-spirited people, but they have all, nevertheless, infused me with courage in my weaker moments.

- Whenever you feel like giving up or just want an extra push forward, close your eyes, take three slow, deep breaths, then recall the faces of your personal winners smiling encouragingly at you.

- Return their smile and, in your imagination, listen to each of them in turn giving you words of encouragement.

- Listen carefully to their words and keep smiling and breathing deeply as you do so. (The smiling and deep breathing will help you to receive the message and fix it in your memory.)

- Close your eyes and listen to your winners' encouragement whenever you need an instant boost of morale.

WORDS OF ENCOURAGEMENT

Here are some quotes from famous people who are/were known for their support of others. Choose one or two right now, close your eyes, relax your body by breathing deeply and listen in your mind to the encouragement that I am sure they would willingly give to you. You don't need to remember the words written here, just let your imagination work spontaneously. Later, you can compile a list of your own mentors to help you.

"Making your mark on the world is hard. If it were easy, everybody would do it. But it's not. It takes patience, it takes commitment and it comes with plenty of failure along the way. The real test is not whether you avoid this failure, because you won't. It's whether you let it harden or shame you into inaction, or whether you learn from it; whether you choose to persevere."

....

Barack Obama, the first black president of the USA

"We can do anything we want as long as we stick to it long enough."

....

Helen Keller, who was left deaf and blind following an illness as a young child; she went on to become a world-famous speaker, author and campaigner for the disabled

"A champion is someone who gets up, even when he can't."

....

Jack Dempsey – the boxer who battled through hardship and poverty to become a legendary world heavyweight champion

"I can stand out the war with any man."

....

Florence Nightingale, who battled against her family, sexism, illness and the establishment to become a pioneering and legendary figure in the world of nursing

"The pain passes, but the beauty remains."

....

Pierre August Rodin, French sculptor, explaining why he still worked when his hands were twisted with arthritis

QUICK FIX:
Have a daily dip into a box full of buzz

This is a favourite with my clients. Fill a box with things that arouse good feelings when you look at, touch, smell or hear them. Here are some ideas:

- Photos of loved ones

- Reminders of your goal and happier times that you are trying to reach

- Shells from a favourite beach

- Pebbles from a rippling brook in a favourite country spot

- A memorable perfume or aromatic oil

- CDs of evocative sounds, such as waves, birds or special songs and music

- Beautiful items of clothing or jewellery

- Small objects/carvings/sculptures

BATTLE WITH ONLY ONE BAD HABIT

·············

When the going gets hard, you are at your most vulnerable to the destructive power of bad habits, and it is so easy at these times to convince yourself that you deserve a break from trying to break them. But what kind of treat is this in reality? You know, in your heart of hearts, that these kinds of habits take both your morale and self-esteem for a nose-dive.

Here are just a few examples of bad habits that can affect morale and slow you down.

- **Discouraging self-talk**

- **Talking negatively about the future to others**

- **Not sticking to helpful routines or "to-do" lists**

- **Watching too much TV**

- **Not eating well (skipping meals, eating fattening or junk food)**

- Going to bed or getting up too late

- Letting good appearance habits slip

- Taking out your temper on people whom you need for support

- Drinking too much alcohol or caffeine

- Skipping energising physical exercise

- Not standing up for yourself when people disrespect you

- Trying to do too much in too little time

Getting the better of all such de-motivating habits is a guaranteed way to boost your morale. But while your life is already heavily pressurised, it makes sense to tackle only one bad habit at any given time.

Once you have chosen your habit, try to alter the way you look at it. View it as the dangerous "enemy" that it actually is. This will make it easier to do battle with it. This is particularly important with the kinds of habit that give you instant pleasure and are therefore a major temptation. When you indulge in habits like these, you tend to feel "mischievous", rather than truly "bad". You may:

- refer to them as "naughty but nice"

- kid yourself that they are a necessary occasional treat – "What's life about, if you can't enjoy yourself once in a while?"

- say, with a cheeky smile, "I'll start tomorrow".

Other people also often find pleasure in seducing you to commit these bad-habit "sins". ("Go on, be a devil . . . it's only this once!") And when others give in to their habits, don't we all feel slightly liberated from our own nagging consciences?

So the battle with a bad habit is often not just with yourself; it can be with your friends too. If this happens, a review of Section 9 will help you with this problem later; but for now, your first priority is to do what you can do. And the exercise below should help you.

You will need a pen and some paper as there are questions that you'll need to answer, and writing down your action points and finding someone to witness your commitment to them will increase your chances of winning the battle. You'll see that some of the questions suggest that a retreat from the battlefield is sometimes advisable. This is because you may need professional help, and it is much better to admit this at an early stage, rather than risk becoming even more demoralised and de-motivated.

"Bad habits are easier to abandon today than tomorrow."

....

Yiddish proverb

PREPARATION FOR A HABIT-BREAKING BATTLE

After choosing your habit, write down the answers to each of the following twelve questions:

1. What do you stand to gain if you win the war with this habit?

For example, you may feel more optimistic and self-confident and better able to move on at a faster rate.

2. What are the conditions that will give your habit an advantage?

This could be tiredness, experiencing a setback, receiving criticism from or being tempted by others.

3. What do you stand to lose if you don't go to war with this habit?

For example, you may become depressed, may not find another job/girlfriend/husband/house, etc.

4. What is your motivating battle slogan?

This could be something like, "My will is stronger than this habit" or, "I can conquer this".

5. What are your battle action goals?

For example:
- "My date for declaring war on this habit is . . ."
- "The date for the first review of my progress is . . ."
- 'The date for the second review of my progress is . . . "

6. How will you keep yourself motivated on a day-to-day basis?

You could, for example, pin these notes up in the kitchen/office; reward yourself each evening with 10 minutes in the bath listening to music and sipping a long, cool drink.

7. Who are your allies and what kind of support can they realistically give you?

For example:

- "John could help me review my progress."
- "Peter could remind me just before I start eating."
- "Both could help me celebrate if I make good progress."

8. What are the warning signs that you might be losing ground in this battle?

For example, if you have given in more than twice in one week.

9. How will I know it is time to retreat and seek more help?

If, for example, your second "battle review" (see above) has revealed that you have given in too many times (if possible, specify the number of failures in a month which, for you, would indicate that it is retreat time).

10. What will you do to obtain help as soon as you declare that you are retreating?

You might, for example, find more people to support you, enrol with a self-help group, see a counsellor or talk to your doctor.

11. How will you celebrate victory?

Take your "allies" out for the night, for example.

12. Who can witness my signature on this declaration?

One of your "allies" might do this.

CHECK THAT YOUR CAPABILITIES MATCH YOUR COMMITMENTS

Thirty-nine-year-old Alice was divorced with two young children. Financially, she was reasonably comfortable as her maintenance payments were supplemented by her part-time work as a book-jacket designer. But her family commitments were quite onerous: her father was suffering from Alzheimer's disease and her mother had had breast cancer and was still very weakened by the treatment. She planned to move to a house with a granny flat for her parents which would ease her child- care difficulties, while at the same time giving her mother, who loves her grandchildren, a positive focus and her father more attention. Although Alice had a circle of supportive friends she felt lonely and missed being part of a couple. She made a resolution to start actively seeking out opportunities to meet a new partner, but six months on, she felt that she was getting nowhere and her morale was at a very low ebb.

One of the first tasks that Alice needed to tackle was to look at how she could cut down on her commitments. It was obvious that she could not manage them in her current state and that things could therefore only get worse for her unless and until she took action.

Over-commitment is one of the most common causes of low morale. A key task for the manager of a successful organisation is to ensure constantly that there is a manageable balance between the capabilities of each member of staff and the commitments that they are expected to meet. This is the exact principle that Alice had to apply to herself in this situation.

Assess the match between your capabilities and commitments

In the table opposite, you'll see that I have identified seven types of capability that are usually needed to handle and keep people going during difficult times (you can change or add to these, if there are others that are more relevant to your situation). To illustrate how this exercise works, I've reproduced Alice's assessment of the match between her own capabilities and commitments. The ticks indicate an OK level of capability in that commitment area.

| | COMMITMENTS | | | | |
CAPABILITIES	Search for a new partner	House move	Childcare	Working life	Mum and Dad support
Physical capacities	X				X
Emotional reserves	X	X	X	X	
Thinking functions			X	X	X
Confidence levels	X	X		X	X
Financial and material resources	X			X	X
Skills/knowledge level			X	X	X
Supply of support	X	X	X	X	

If your assessment reveals an imbalance, you will need to cut down on your commitments, delegate aspects of them or improve your capability. Alice's notes (below) will give you an idea of how this can be done.

ALICE'S ACTION NOTES

1. Should postpone plans to move house.

2. To boost me emotionally I need to spend more quality time with Fiona [her best friend] – perhaps we could go on weekend retreat together when ex- comes over from the States in the summer.

3. Not thinking very creatively at work but can coast OK for a while longer. Break should help.

4. Must give myself an urgent confidence boost (Section 2 of this book).

5. Ring social worker at the hospital next week and see if I can get home nursing support for Mum and Dad.

6. Perhaps can start to find out more about dating agen- cies, even though my capabilities are way too low to start yet.

I am only one
But still I am one
I cannot do everything
But I can do something

. . . .

Edward Everett Hale,
author and statesman

QUICK FIX:
Permit pauses in your progress

Moving on from hard times rarely goes forward consistently. There will be setbacks and periods when nothing appears to be happening. You need to accept this and plan ahead as to how you will use any such "waiting" time constructively.

Being self-employed, I've had to learn how to do this. I keep certain administrative office work and house-maintenance tasks for such low-activity periods. Also, on birthdays and at Christmas, my husband often gives me a present of a day in a spa. These will be filed away and used during one of the fallow periods in my work schedule. Another favourite filler activity of mine is to do some catching up with friends.

Why not apply the same principle to the dips in your momentum? Think of positive tasks you could do should you encounter a setback or have to wait around for finance or someone to do something before you can step forward again. Then, instead of feeling fed up, you will find yourself saying, "Great – this gives me a chance to catch up on/learn/finish/start.."

POWER YOURSELF INTO ACTION WITH GOALS

. . . .

"First say to yourself what you would be; and then do what you have to do."

. . . .

Epictetus, Greek philosopher

Epictetus was born into slavery and suffered many setbacks in his life (including physical disability and exile), yet he became one of mankind's most influential philosophers. The wisdom that he imparted concerning personal power is as relevant today for anyone who is encountering tough times as it ever was.

Epictetus believed that the key to recovery is to use your personal power effectively. So rather than focusing on those aspects of what has happened to you that were, or are, beyond your control, you should deal with something that is within your power to change – namely, yourself and your attitudes. So now is the time to give your momentum a real push forward by making some resolutions to use your personal power in the most effective ways that you can. Goal setting is crucial for this, but only if it is done well.

First, you must have a long-term dream that is challenging enough to inspire you, but realistic enough to ensure that you have a fair chance of realising it. Next, you need a series of step-by-step objectives with deadlines to give you a sense of achievement and an opportunity for some well-deserved rewards along the way. The following exercise will help you to put this theory into action and to firm up your commitment to keeping your morale as high as it possibly can be in difficult times.

YOUR GOAL-SETTING PLAN OF ACTION

Fill in the blank spaces in the statements below. Try to do this exercise now or at least by the end of the day or tomorrow, at the latest. You can always write in pencil and make changes later if necessary, but you will get an instant boost from doing some goal-setting immediately.

1. In five years' time I intend to be able to look back at this period and feel . (For example, "a sense of achievement", "inner peace", "in control", etc.)

2. In five years' time I intend to . (For example, "be doing more work that satisfies me", "have established a support group to help others in the same situation", "be living happily with a new partner", etc.)

3. By the end of next year I will have . (For example, "conquered my fear", "be driving again", "paid off the loan from my mother", etc.)

4. In six months' time I will have . (For example, "signed up with a dating agency if I haven't met anyone", "chosen a couple of alternative career options", etc.)

5. In one month's time, I will have . (For example, "seen a debt consultant", "improved my sleep regime", etc.)

6. The three tips in this book that I will reread and use immediately to give me the morale boost I need are:

A FINAL WORD

As you must have gathered from reading this book, my own life has been peppered with all manner of setbacks. However, I know that there are many other difficulties that I could have faced and there may be even more just around the corner.

And you too may be aware – and fearful – of the "unknown". Perhaps you are even thinking along these lines right now, and feeling sceptical about the future, despite having read through this collection of tips. But I hope that you will soon start to put many of them into action in earnest, because when you do, you will start to feel differently. Then, in the future, should your self-confidence and trust in the world be knocked back again, you will find that the skills you have acquired for recovering your psycho- logical power will automatically flip back into the forefront of your mind.

Most importantly, this will be true even when you cannot improve your physical or material circumstances. It was only when this happened to me personally – when my daughter Laura was killed – that I believed this could really be so. During this period, I used to repeat the following Chinese proverb to myself: "You cannot prevent the birds of **sadness** from flying over your head, but you can prevent them from nesting in your hair." I have taken the liberty of highlighting the word "sadness" here because I have found that it can be replaced with other emotions that affect morale negatively during difficult times (such as guilt, jealousy or anger), so that the proverb's wisdom can be applied in many situations.

Finally, perhaps once you are feeling stronger in yourself, you will pass on your new knowledge and insight to anyone else who may be struggling to stay positive through problem situations. Not only will this give them much needed comfort and encouragement, it will also strengthen your own morale further still.

So, good luck – and I hope that armed with the knowledge of *How to Feel Good in Difficult Times*, you'll find your recovery is quicker than you'd ever dreamed possible.

TriggerHub.org is one of the most elite and scientifically proven forms of mental health intervention

Trigger Publishing is the leading independent mental health and wellbeing publisher in the UK and US. Clinical and scientific research conducted by assistant professor Dr Kristin Kosyluk and her highly acclaimed team in the Department of Mental Health Law & Policy at the University of South Florida (USF), as well as complementary research by her peers across the US, has independently verified the power of lived experience as a core component in achieving mental health prosperity. Specifically, the lived experiences contained within our bibliotherapeutic books are intrinsic elements in reducing stigma, making those with poor mental health feel less alone, providing the privacy they need to heal, ensuring they know the essential steps to kick-start their own journeys to recovery, and providing hope and inspiration when they need it most.

Delivered through TriggerHub, our unique online portal and accompanying smartphone app, we make our library of bibliotherapeutic titles and other vital resources accessible to individuals and organizations anywhere, at any time and with complete privacy, a crucial element of recovery. As such, TriggerHub is the primary recommendation across the UK and US for the delivery of lived experiences.

At Trigger Publishing and TriggerHub, we proudly lead the way in making the unseen become seen. We are dedicated to humanizing mental health, breaking stigma and challenging outdated societal values to create real action and impact. Find out more about our world-leading work with lived experience and bibliotherapy via triggerhub.org, or by joining us on:

🐦 @triggerhub_

📘 @triggerhub.org

📷 @triggerhub_

Printed in the USA
CPSIA information can be obtained
at www.ICGtesting.com
JSHW031713140824
68134JS00038B/3664